Big Gardens in Small Spaces

Big Gardens in Small Spaces

Out-of-the-Box Advice for Boxed-in Gardeners

Martyn Cox

Timber Press
Portland | London

Frontispiece: Plan carefully to make the most of the available space. In this scene, walls, raised beds and even the steps down into the garden have been planted up, still allowing room for a tiny lawn and patio. Photograph by Andrew Lawson, courtesy of The Garden Collection.

Photographs are by the author unless otherwise indicated.

Published in 2009 by Timber Press, Inc.

The Haseltine Building
133 S.W. Second Avenue, Suite 450
Portland, Oregon 97204-3527
www.timberpress.com

2 The Quadrant
135 Salusbury Road
London NW6 6RJ
www.timberpress.co.uk

ISBN-13: 978-0-88192-907-2

Printed in China

Library of Congress Cataloguing-in-Publication Data

Cox, Martyn.
Big gardens in small spaces : out-of-the-box advice for boxed-in gardeners / Martyn Cox. — 1st ed.
p. cm.
Includes bibliographical references and index.
ISBN 978-0-88192-907-2
1. Small gardens—Design. I. Title.
SB473.C695 2009
635.9'67—dc22

2009022892

A catalogue record for this book is also available from the British Library.

For Alis, Louis and Lily

Contents

Introduction   9

1. Don't Mind the Gaps   31

2. Going Up   65

3. Just Eat It   89

4. Taming Monsters   123

5. Seasonal Stars   143

6. Colour Code   159

7. How to Keep the Small Garden Going   173

The Plants in My Garden   197

Resources   202

Index   209

Introduction

JEALOUSY IS A TERRIBLE sin, but I'm going to come clean straight away and admit that I'm often envious when I visit a garden much larger than the tiny patch I own. Not every big garden triggers my shameful green gene, of course, but there are plenty that do. Generally they are two acres or more, and divided into a series of rooms, each with a distinctive look. Among the features you might find are a kitchen garden bursting at the seams with good things to eat, a substantial water feature, lawns, deep filled borders, a little bit of woodland and an outdoor dining area. Oh, and they are probably attached to a fabulous house and have the kind of view that leaves you breathless.

Yet, as the old adage goes, size isn't everything, and I truly believe you can have an exciting, attractive, productive, usable and plant-filled space, even if you can step out of the back door of your house and almost touch the rear wall of your garden with an outstretched arm.

Sadly, though, I think many people feel hamstrung by their tiny garden and fail to create anything that gets anywhere near setting the pulse racing. For evidence, board a train and put down your book or stop fiddling with your MP3 player while it travels through an urban area—you will see many private backyards or gardens where the owner has done little, or sometimes absolutely nothing, to stamp their mark on the plot. There are many examples where I live, in Walthamstow, East London. I call them identikit—formulaic—gardens because they are replicas of each other, from the types of plants used to the very simple structure that gives the garden its backbone.

Opposite: No garden? No problem. The owners of this cottage have made the most of the entrance to their home with lots of colourful plants in pots.

9

Broadly, these Victorian terraced houses have a rectangular plot at the back that consists of a lawn bisected by a path leading to a garden shed. The plants, if there are any, consist of hard-wearing, low-maintenance, utilitarian shrubs that are usually seen gracing the kind of landscape scheme you would see around the perimeter of a supermarket. Yes, the result is a garden that is functional, but it looks dull, dull, dull and is largely used for hanging up the washing, having a barbecue or letting children or pets take some exercise.

The failure to do anything with a small garden depresses, irritates and dumbfounds me in just about equal measures. I really can't understand why no attempt has been made to transform the space into something that will delight all of your senses every time you step out the back door.

As a garden writer, and owner of a small garden, I have written many features over the years that have tried to encourage those with tiny plots to make the most of what they have. Being starved of space is really no excuse for a humdrum plot, and a tiny garden does not have to be short on ideas.

I have seen many inspirational balconies, terraces, patios and postage-stamp-sized front and back gardens while travelling around the United Kingdom. For instance, I once visited an unusual garden in rural Nottinghamshire, in the heart of the Midlands, where the space at the front was a dead ringer for a seaside garden. For many years this had been lawn, but the owner had a 'road to Damascus' moment while visiting Beth Chatto's famous gravel garden in Essex. Soon after, the lawn was stripped away and 11 tonnes of gravel spread over the soil, with different grades of pebbles arranged in swathes to create interesting textural shapes. Into this sea of shingle he had planted perennials, such as *Sanguisorba*, *Sisyrinchium* and *Libertia*, along with many ornamental grasses, including *Miscanthus*, *Briza maxima*, *Stipa gigantea* and *Hordeum jubatum*. To dampen this dry landscape, a stream was built that runs into a shimmering pond, whose margins were planted with equisetum, primulas and hostas. To finish, driftwood was dragged up from the nearby River Trent and arranged among the plants.

Equally uplifting, but totally different in its look, was a tiny city-centre plot. At the back of a nineteenth-century house at 28 Kensington Road in Bristol, on the west coast of England, was a space measuring just 20 ft. by 18 ft., where the owners had built a terrific garden that had been divided into two rooms and then filled with hundreds of plants (they didn't know exactly how many) that had knitted together to completely envelope you. Taking their cue from large, stately gardens, they had then built 'domains' such as a formal garden, an exotic garden, a herb garden, a pond, a temple folly ruin, a rock garden and a lawn.

Of course, each of these areas was minuscule and the execution often carried out with a great deal of humour: the lawn consisted of some grass growing in a pot,

Opposite: The edges of this narrow passageway have been crammed full of plants, leaving just enough room to reach a comfortable chair. Photograph by Derek St Romaine, courtesy of The Garden Collection.

A front garden doesn't have to be just a functional way to reach the front door. A quirky recycled-wood fence and architectural plants such as *Pseudopanax crassifolius* turn entering the house into a memorable experience. Photograph by Jonathan Buckley, courtesy of The Garden Collection.

Opposite: My tiny garden in June.

A dull front garden has been transformed with a seaside planting scheme.

Grasses and drought-resistant perennials knit together beautifully and thrive with very little care.

with a toy lawnmower placed on top and a 'keep off the grass' sign nearby, while the herb garden was simply small pots of herbs arranged in a wire basket. Other features within the garden were more substantial. The formal garden was a collection of clipped topiary arranged beneath a classical statue, and the exotic garden was a fiery planting of cannas, dahlias and other hot-coloured perennials. It was a truly eclectic garden, and on paper you would have thought that the ingredients that had gone into making it would doom it to failure. The opposite was the case. It worked fantastically well and is testament to the skill and imagination of the owners.

It's even possible to make a garden in the most unlikely of places. A walk along the South Bank of the River Thames, from Tower Bridge towards Bermondsey, will

The garden at 28 Kensington Road in Bristol, England, is the smallest open for the National Gardens Scheme and has been filled with hundreds of plants grown in pots.

Garden too small for a lawn? This proves it's possible to have a verdant sward whatever space you have.

A crumbling classical arch rising above formal clipped box is among an eclectic range of features found in the tiny garden at 28 Kensington Road.

The pint-sized tops of barges moored on the River Thames in London make perfect floating gardens.

Sunflowers planted in a row help to soften the stark architecture of the cityscape and are testament to the inhabitant's skill in creating a garden where no soil is present.

lead you to a place known locally as Garden Barge Square—a collection of six barges moored on the river which have had their tops planted up. They look amazing and are ample proof that whatever the amount of space you have, you can still grow some plants. One of the barges has been planted with trees, another with perennials, grasses and architectural shrubs, while in late summer I spotted a striking barge with a wall of sunflowers on top.

The ideas behind these and other gardens, including my own, will be looked at in detail within the pages of this book. There are suggestions for making the most of boundary fences or walls, the walls of a garden structure or even those of your house. These vertical surfaces are often forgotten about, left naked of any vegetation, but they can support so many wonderful plants, from self-clinging climbers to shrubs that need a bit more support. During times when we are trying to save money on our weekly shopping bills or aiming to reduce our carbon footprint, they can also be used for growing fruit or even vegetables, such as courgettes (zucchini), squash or gourds.

Filling gaps, whether in beds, under shrubs, around the bare leg of a tree in a pot or where the mortar has worked itself loose between paving slabs, is at the heart of this book. I have suggested numerous plants that will work well within a confined space, including many plants I have grown myself, from hardy annuals to fruit, vegetables, perennials, bulbs and shrubs that will lift any tiny garden.

One key to planting a small garden is to learn how to manipulate plants. Possessing a few feet of growing space does not mean you have to stick to growing compact, dwarf or restricted forms of plants, or shrubs that resemble stunted bonsais. Pruning large-leaved plants or harnessing their growth by putting them in a pot means you can grow some pretty impressive beasts, and training plants against wires means you can grow fruit plants that are normally seen as free-standing trees.

Even soilless parts of the garden can play their part in the bigger picture. It is possible to grow lots of plants in a redundant corner, deep windowsill or balcony, or to hide an ugly feature, simply by creating a stage for the plants. It is something I have done for many years, arranging plants (in their pots) together to make an attractive display and building up the height by placing them on top of each other or by raising them up on upturned pots. If the pots remain hidden, the results can be stunning, and you can change the display whenever the plants demand it or the mood takes you.

This is most definitely not a book on how to design a small garden—there are plenty of those—but a guide to planting a small garden and squeezing more plants into your space by making the most of every surface, gap, fissure or pot. Here is my personal manifesto:

Planting in raised beds is an ideal way of growing specialty plants. Here, Japanese maple, heathers and azaleas grow in a bed filled with ericaceous compost, in a garden that naturally has alkaline soil. Photograph by Nicola Stocken Tomkins, courtesy of The Garden Collection.

Clearly seen from the windows of the house, this small garden full of exotics has been designed as a leafy retreat from the chaotic world outside the front door. Photograph by Jonathan Buckley, courtesy of The Garden Collection.

I AM FOR

Squeezing as many plants as you can into the garden by any means
   possible

Welcoming wildlife

Growing your own fruit, vegetables and herbs—they taste good, save
   money and allow you to grow plants that aren't available in shops

Seeking out rare, unusual and bizarre plants to grow

Change

The slow development of the garden through experience and the
   absorbing of new ideas

Enjoying the garden and having fun

The DIY ethic—don't pay for something you can make or do yourself

Learning from nature

Recycling what you can

I AM AGAINST

Minimalism in the garden

Credit card gardening

Hiring a gardener to maintain your space

Inert gardens

Monocultures

Manicured lawns

Liberal use of chemicals

Identikit small gardens—the lawn, path and shed combo (yuck!)

Overly zealous garden maintenance—laboratory conditions outdoors will
   result in a sterile space

Too many bedding plants

Some of the ideas you will read about may not be suitable for your garden, but many will be, and others could be adapted to work with what you have. Even if you do not follow my advice to the letter, what you read about may be the spark that leads you to try something new and creative. And that can only be a good thing for you and your garden.

How my tiny garden started

When my family (partner, Alis, and two children, Louis and Lily) and I moved into our Victorian terrace house in East London, we inherited an uninspiring, boring, unkempt and tiny back garden. The 30 ft. by 15 ft. rectangular space consisted of a meagre patio of ugly red and grey concrete paving slabs at the head of a lawn composed more of muddy and weedy patches than actual blades of grass. Running down either side were some thin borders planted with a motley assortment of shrubs that had not seen a pair of secateurs (pruning shears) for years—there were a couple of roses, a lilac, a rosemary and near the back of the house, blocking out much of the available light, a towering rhododendron whose canopy reached the upstairs windows of the house. In the bottom left-hand corner of the garden was a shed, painted Barleywood blue (de rigueur in every outdoor space in the United Kingdom during the late 1990s and early 2000s thanks to the popular gardening programme *Ground Force*), which had seen much better days but was just about still standing.

There was nothing remarkable about this garden at all, but I wanted a blank canvas where I could make my mark, and I could see the potential in this plot. It faced due south, which meant I could grow many of the sun-loving exotics that I was passionate about at the time, and it would be perfect for barbecues, alfresco meals and simply lounging about in the sun.

Even before we moved into the house, I had started to put some design plans down on paper. They would change often, sometimes daily, as a new idea came into my head, but the one thing that never changed was my aim to cram the garden to the gunnels with my favourite plants. This desire was partly based on my obsession with plants, which I collected (and still collect) with the same enthusiasm that I do vinyl records, old toys, vintage comic books and other treasures that my partner cruelly describes as 'tat'.

The plant-filled garden that I planned to create would be the antithesis of many small gardens that I visit as a garden writer. So often I see gardens, smaller or slightly bigger than mine, that are minimalist extensions of the home, where a few low-maintenance plants exist around structural, stark hard landscaping. Although I can appreciate the aesthetics of a garden like this, where smooth lines are rarely interrupted by plants, it's not very interesting to a plant lover like myself and not the kind of space where I want to linger for any length of time.

Although the house was a bit of a wreck and needed a new kitchen and bathroom, decorating, floors sanded and shelves put in, along with a long list of more minor improvements, the first thing I did was tackle the garden. Well, why not? Writing about gardens is what I do for a living, so it seemed obvious to start the overhaul of the property outside.

Opposite: There's not a scrap of soil here, but the walls, windowsill and even a potting bench have been made to work hard, supporting a collection of plants grown in containers. Photograph by Nicola Stocken Tomkins, courtesy of The Garden Collection.

Rather than work with what I had, I instigated a scorched earth policy. A spade easily peeled the scrappy lawn from the ground, the smaller shrubs were unceremoniously hoicked out of the ground and I took great pleasure in reducing the dilapidated shed to kindling within minutes. All it took was a few whacks with a heavy-duty sledgehammer.

That left the rhododendron. I put aside a weekend and started by cutting off branches until I was eventually left with a stump that reminded me of the kind of sculpture you often see in a museum of classical antiquities—one that, following several centuries of mistreatment, is left without arms, legs or perhaps even a head. With the easy bit over, it was time to remove the stump. This was hard work—the tree had been happily romping away for at least fifty years. I needed help and enlisted my dad and brother. You would have thought three men would have easily wrestled the stump from the ground, but it was firmly anchored and the roots deep. Still, we dug, rocked it, dug, chopped, dug, sawed, scraped and swore until we eventually hoisted it free of the soil.

My plan for the now empty plot was simple. First, a fence would be installed on three sides for privacy and to provide vertical surfaces for plants. I would keep the patio (and replace it with nicer stone when I could afford to) and put a curved slate shingle path down the centre that would lead to a small timber deck. To make the

My shed had seen much better days and was no match for a sledgehammer.
Photograph by Paul Cox.

garden more interesting and add some structure, I would edge one side of the path with sleepers (railroad ties), cut to different sizes and erected lengthways to make a curved wall. The spaces on either side of the path would become borders.

A greenhouse was essential for propagation and housing tender plants, so I found the smallest model that I could still walk into comfortably and erected it opposite the deck. Next to it, in the redundant right-hand corner of the garden, I fitted a small shed for storing tools and bags of compost. As you can never have enough space to stow away garden clutter, I built a brick storage seat between the patio and the left-hand bed. It's ideal. You can sit on it, put things in it and even arrange plants on top of it.

Putting the 'bones' of the garden together went fairly smoothly, but there was the occasional hiccup. One memorable incident occurred when I was preparing the soil for laying the deck. After a few minutes excavating there was an audible clang as my spade hit something metallic. I scraped away at the soil until a curved outline was visible. My dad, who was helping me at the time, probed at the object with a garden cane. I urged caution and asked my elderly neighbour if incendiary devices had fallen on the area during the Second World War. He confirmed they had, so the police were called. Within minutes two officers appeared, followed shortly after by their boss. We were ordered to the front room of the house and the street was

This slate-floored patio at the back of my house is ideal for chilling out after a hard day writing or for taking time out from gardening.

Opposite: A curved slate shingle path leads to a deck under a shade sail.

Poppy, our overweight and mature cat, takes it easy on my garden's sleeper wall.

cordoned off. Soon the bomb disposal squad arrived in their Land Rover and entered the back garden armed with spades. Half an hour or so later, I was summoned outside by one of the team. His partner stood in the garden holding the bomb in his hand, smiling widely—it was an old galvanized bucket. Yes, I was extremely embarrassed, but it's given me a story that I've been able to dine out on for years.

After finishing the hard landscaping I was able to start thinking about planting. I had amassed a huge collection of plants over the years, some of which had followed me from one rented property to another in their pots and others that my parents had kindly allowed me to store in their garden. Now it was time for their liberation. First I improved the heavy clay soil that is common to much of London. As many of my plants were sun lovers with a hankering for that tricky combination of moisture-retentive but well-drained soil, I added lots of horticultural grit (1–4 mm fine gravel) to open it up, along with several bags of well-rotted farmyard manure.

With the two borders planted, I was itching to squeeze more plants into the garden and looked at ways I could achieve my goal. Fences became supports for fruit, climbers and climbing shrubs, while plants in pots were pushed up against the sun-baked walls of my house. Although this made great use of the vertical space, some of the pots took up a lot of room, so I started to think about how I could fill the space below. In some cases I would underplant the tree with a low-growing plant or

Gardening is all about compromise. Even in a small, plant-filled garden it's important to give your children some space for their toys.

arrange other plants on top of the compost in their pots. In my quest to grow more, I planted up gaps that would normally be left unfilled and conjured up ways of growing lots of plants in the same pot, whether this was a collection of carnivorous plants in a large container or a dozen or so alpines in an old ceramic sink.

As a keen cook and lover of fresh fruit and vegetables, I wanted a garden that would be productive as well as ornamental. Although I have no pretensions about becoming self-sufficient, I wanted to grow enough of my own produce to contribute towards meals and to show my children where food comes from. While many edibles are greedy for space, plenty can be grown in pots, trained against wires or elbowed between other plants in the border. Apart from traditional varieties, I also sought out new plants bred specifically for growing where space is stretched.

Although I had a broad plan for the structure when I first started work on my garden, I continually honed the elements within it. A visit to the countryside, where I would observe how plants cling to the walls farmers erect to divide fields, might furnish me with a notion for planting up the vertical plane of a garden wall. Trips to gardens of all sizes were equally productive, providing me with plenty of ideas to steal. On the other hand, something that I thought might work sometimes proved to be a complete failure and had to be abandoned.

For the first few years the garden looked like exactly what it was—a newly planted garden with plants a fraction of the size they would eventually become. But from the third summer onwards, it became the space I had always hoped it would be. The plants within it were firmly established and had knitted together so well that when you walked down the garden path you felt completely secluded and hidden from all the neighbouring houses.

Of course I continue to find ways to squeeze more plants in, and from a purely selfish point of view, I would be happy to completely fill the patio and deck. However, many gardens are a compromise between what the main gardener wants and the needs of everybody else sharing the space. And my garden is no different. Two young children need to be able to play, and having room for dining outdoors allows us all to get together and enjoy this big garden thriving in a small space.

1
Don't Mind the Gaps

'MIND THE GAP' is a phrase that anyone who has travelled on London's underground rail system will instantly recognize. The recorded message is repeated several times as the train pulls to a stop, warning of the hazardous cleft between the carriage and platform. Well, this chapter is not about avoiding gaps but about embracing every chink, fissure, crevice, hole, bare patch, nook and cranny in your garden.

I'm not surprised that gaps are some of the most underused spaces in the garden, as they can sometimes be tricky to plant up and are often seen as too much of a challenge. Not only do you have to establish the plant, you also have to find varieties that will thrive in these difficult areas. However, by making the most of every gap, you will greatly increase the number of plants in your garden and be able to grow some varieties that you really couldn't grow anywhere else.

When planting, aim to find some exciting, rare or unusual varieties, or combine plants to make a striking display, and avoid the temptation to stick to hackneyed choices for your gaps. For instance, I love tiny-leaved, mat-forming Corsican mint (*Mentha requienii*), New Zealand burr (*Acaena microphylla* 'Kupferteppich') with its fuzzy red flower-heads and ground-hugging thymes, such as *Thymus serpyllum* 'Pink Chintz', *T. pseudolanuginosus* and *T.* Coccineus Group, but if I see them planted in another patio I might give up the will to live. Yes, some have a fantastic scent when crushed underfoot, yes, some can put up with a certain amount of foot traffic and yes, some have pretty flowers, but there are many other plants that would grow equally as well, look far less one-dimensional and possess bags more ooh la la.

Perhaps the most inspiring and experimental gap planting on a patio that I

Opposite: Purple irises make a bold statement with other perennials in Francesca Murray's garden. Photograph by Francesca Murray.

31

have ever seen was the work of Francesca Murray, a garden designer based in Buckinghamshire, England. When she moved to a new home, she inherited a garden with a mundane sea of paving slabs and decided to turn it into a feature by removing the occasional slab to create some planting pockets. She really crammed each pocket with plants, using a mixture of spring bulbs, perennials and grasses to make a vibrant, vertical display that has something of interest all year round, whether it's flowers, seed heads or evergreen foliage. Among the plants were choice grasses, such as *Pennisetum thunbergii* 'Red Buttons' and *Miscanthus sinensis* 'Ferner Osten', which rubbed shoulders with purple sedum, *Eupatorium*, *Sisyrinchium*, *Echinacea*, *Bergenia* and sage. Even though the gaps were fairly compact, she managed to grow a staggering amount of plants, proving that prostrate plants are not the only solution for gaps in a patio.

This example of adventurous planting should help to inspire anyone wanting to make the most of gap filling, whether it's a garden wall, house wall, path, patio or an awkward spot under another plant.

Garden walls

The county of Cornwall, in the far south-west corner of England, is famed for its dramatic coastline, but head inland and you'll find countryside that is equally as breathtaking. Here you will find miles of walls, which fan out like arteries to divide land, provide shelter from the wind that whips in off the sea, muffle sound or mark the side of a road. These walls, confusingly known as Cornish hedges, are sometimes very old (there are examples dating back to the fifteenth century, although most were built two hundred years ago), but there has been a renaissance in building these unique structures, and you can walk around many modern housing developments where these walls have been built as a boundary to separate the front garden from the road.

So why have I included Cornish hedges in a book about planting up a small garden? Well, that's simple. They have been designed with the intention of becoming home to a rich selection of plants and are not just a functional enclosure. Their construction and style, plus the opportunity they give to grow lots more plants, should be considered by anyone wanting to build a new garden wall.

Made from local stone, walls are usually laid dry and are double thickness, allowing the central core to be filled with soil. Plants can then be planted into the soil on top of the wall, squeezed into the gaps between the stones that make up the vertical sides and planted at the base. Cornish hedges are perfect for a front gar-

Grape hyacinths carpet
a wall in spring in a
Cornish street.

den wall, although their width precludes their use as an internal dividing wall in very small gardens.

In rural locations, walls are usually completely cloaked with mosses, liverworts, native flowers, grasses and bulbs, while the top is planted with hedgerow trees, such as common hawthorn (*Crataegus monogyna*) and blackthorn (*Prunus spinosa*). When a wall is built as a boundary for a garden, it is possible to be far more creative. You will often see the top planted with *Fuchsia* 'Riccartonii', escallonias, small rambler roses, *Berberis darwinii* and tamarix, with an underplanting of spring bulbs, such as muscari, daffodils and multi-coloured hyacinths, which exude a potent scent that will delight anyone who happens to be passing by.

The sides of the wall can be colonized with a mixture of ready-grown plants, plugs and seeds. There are many that are suitable. The wonderful *Erigeron karvinskia-*

Bulbs provide a bold splash of colour in spring when planted in the tops of walls.

A flash of buttery yellow caught my eye when driving along a country lane in spring. This primrose (*Primula vulgaris*) is a great example of how plants self-seed in nature.

Erigeron daisies self-seed freely and cloak the sides of a wall at Logan Botanical Garden in Scotland.

Small ferns have been planted in wall crevices at Chesters Walled Garden in Northumberland.

Thymes planted together on the top of a dry stone wall at Rosemoor.

nus (Mexican fleabane), which thrives in drought conditions and forms a mat of foliage studded with white and pink daisies, will spread happily and looks great with the starry lavender flowers of *Campanula poscharskyana*, a native of the mountainous regions of eastern Europe. Ferns are perfect, as are delicate grasses such as bents and fescues. For a more organic look, allow nature to have a hand in creating the spectacle—don't be too rigorous about removing plants that have self-seeded.

Although a mixture of different plants is appealing, there is no reason why a wall could not be used for a specific type of plant, such as edible crops. The top would be ideal for dwarf forms of gooseberry or upright herbs, such as chives, while wild or cultivated strawberries would thrive in the gaps between stones on the vertical face. A good alternative would be to grow alpines. At the Royal Horticultural Society's garden at Rosemoor in Devon, the top of a chest-high wall has been adorned with these diminutive plants, arranged among a sea of grit to keep the base of each plant dry. Among the plants are *Campanula portenschlagiana*, *Sisyrinchium* 'Californian Skies', *Geranium subcaulescens*, *Dianthus* 'Calypso Star', *Veronica austriaca* 'Ionian Skies' and *Phlox stolonifera* compact. The height of the wall makes it perfect for observing these miniature marvels up close and personal.

Stone walls, similar to those found in Cornwall, have long been used to make a garden more attractive or to provide a habit for special plants. In *The English Flower Garden*, first published in 1883, William Robinson described making a dry stone wall of sandstone. After each stone was laid, he placed an alpine plant in a gap, covered the roots with sand or soil, then laid another stone. He observed that many alpines, which would have rotted with their feet in wet soil over winter, thrived in the wall. Among the plants he grew were *Armeria*, dwarf forms of *Dierama*, alpine wall-flowers, *Linaria* and dwarf gentians.

Gertrude Jekyll was another advocate of growing in a wall. Within the pages of *Wood and Garden*, from 1899, she goes into great detail about how she created a double dry stone wall with a core of earth at her Munstead Wood garden. One side was planted with *Blechnum*, *Polypodium* and *Adiantum* ferns, while shrub roses, *Berberis*, junipers, *Ribes* and *Olearia* ×*haastii* grew in the soil on top, giving it an overall height of 10 ft. (3 m) in places.

Although stone walls look beautiful, they are really only suitable for a rural location, and in towns or cities walls are generally made from bricks of the same stock as your house. The use of mortar to bind bricks together means there aren't lots of vertical gaps that can be planted up (although yellow *Corydalis lutea* and *Buddleja davidii* managed to self-seed in the unpointed gaps of my old front wall, which has subsequently been replaced by a new one built from reclaimed bricks), but I have still seen some gardeners find clever ways to customize an ordinary brick wall to boost the number of plants they can grow.

A neighbour of mine has an urban version of the Cornish hedge. Well, kind of. It's a double-thickness red brick wall with a compost infill, perfect for a selection of alpines to flourish. However, perhaps the most exuberant front garden wall I've ever seen is owned by Don Mapp, a native of Belize who now lives in East London. In the middle of summer, Don's front wall is completely cloaked behind a tapestry of flowers, leaves and seed heads. The secret to this? A length of plastic guttering has been attached to the back of the wall and filled with compost that now supports sedums, red verbena, mini-petunias, fuchsias and quaking grass, underplanted with bulbs such as the double-flowered *Colchicum* 'Waterlily' to give interest in mid-autumn. Tumbling down the face of the wall is a bright orange black-eyed Susan (*Thunbergia alata*) which is trained along a series of wires that have been secured to

This urban wall in Don Mapp's London garden has a length of guttering behind it that supports a zingy mixture of plants.

the wall. Don has also created two planting holes in the middle of the wall—several bricks have been knocked out and the void filled with two large terracotta pots that have been placed on their sides. A mixture of general-purpose potting compost and a handful of controlled-release fertilizer has been added to the containers, which have been planted with *Clematis* 'Rouge Cardinal', nasturtium, bacopa and petunia.

House walls

Long journeys by train sap my energy like nothing else. Within a few minutes of boarding the 8:00 a.m. from King's Cross station in London to Edinburgh Waverly station, or even more gruelling, the 7:30 a.m. from London's Paddington station to Penzance in Cornwall, I start to feel light-headed and my eyes flicker with tiredness. Strange, because I feel perfectly chipper before the electric doors close. Yes, I know it's a peculiar reaction to travelling by public transport, but I can't bear sitting still for too long and am greatly relieved when I finally reach my destination. At last I have the opportunity to do something meaningful with my day.

Still, there are advantages, for a garden writer, to travelling across the country by train. Whenever it slows down to pass through a town or city, you get a great glimpse of the denizens' back gardens, and on a trip that lasts several hours, you can see hundreds of these private spaces. Some are beautifully planted, others boast only a few token shrubs, while a fair few have been laid to a lawn that has been lost under a blanket of brightly coloured kids' toys.

And yet there is something that unifies most of these gardens—an expanse of unadorned bricks that rises up to form the back wall of the house. When you see a lot of properties in quick succession you can't help but notice all this vacant space, and apart from an occasional token clematis, wisteria or Boston ivy, these structural walls are largely deficient of greenery.

Although the walls of your house present more of a challenge to plant up than any other surface, they should certainly be considered, especially if your garden is tiny or if the only outdoor space you have is a balcony attached to a flat.

For encouragement look no further than Patrick Blanc, an innovative French garden designer who has become renowned for a technique he calls *Le Mur Végétal*, or The Vertical Garden. Inspired by the way in which plants anchor themselves on rocks, tree trunks and slopes in the wild, without the need for soil, Blanc set about devising a system for growing plants vertically that would ape what he witnessed in nature.

His technique for greening a wall starts with hanging a metal frame on the chosen surface and then attaching a waterproof layer of 1 cm thick PVC sheet. A rot-proof polyamide felt sheet is then stapled to the PVC. Seeds, cuttings or ready-grown plants are introduced to the felt, and the roots soon become embedded on the surface or between the fibres. The felt is kept moist by a computerized irrigation system that supplies water and nutrients from above.

The system is foolproof and can be adapted anywhere. All Blanc has to do is tailor the choice of plants he uses, depending on the climate in the part of the world where he is working. His walls embellish hotels, museums, car parks, apartment blocks and private homes across the world, including the Musée du quai Branly in Paris, New York's Phyto Universe spa, La Bastide restaurant in Los Angeles and the French Embassy in New Delhi.

Blanc's system is technically advanced and usually executed on a large scale, but there is no reason why a similar technique could not be attempted on the wall of a typical house. For example, sedum matting, which is normally supplied in sheets or rolls for making green roofs, can be hung vertically. I've seen this put into practice by leading garden designer Stephen Woodhams, who covered an area of wall at his offices in London with sedum matting embellished with other plants. To do this, a steel frame was attached to an outside wall, followed by a water-retentive mat and then a sheet of sedum matting held in place with wire mesh. An irrigation system was then set up, which supplied water from the top of the frame.

This panel of greenery looked great as it provided verdant colour all year round, along with flowers in the spring and summer. The geo-textile matting was planted with seven different sedums: *Sedum spurium*, *S. album*, *S. rupestre*, *S. kamtschaticum*, *S. pulchellum*, *S. sexangulare* and *S. acre*. Planting pockets were then gouged out and ferns and other plants added, among them hart's tongue fern (*Asplenium scolopendrium*), fishtail fern (*Cyrtomium falcatum*) and *Sedum* 'Autumn Joy'.

Not all living walls are soilless. The Canadian company ELT (Elevated Landscape Technologies) has devised a product called the Easy Green Living Wall, a modular panel made from UV-resistant, high-density polythene (polyethylene) and filled with a water-retentive compost mix. The panel is divided up into a grid, resulting in a number of large, square planting cells. The bottom of each is angled downward slightly to prevent the compost from falling out.

Planting it up is easy. Place the panel on a flat surface and fill each cell to the top with compost, packing it down firmly with your hands. Plants can then be placed in the compost, firmed in hard, watered and then firmed again. If you are using established plants, the panel can be erected straightaway, but if you are using seeds or plugs, it is best to keep the panel horizontal until they have had a chance to establish.

The choice of what to grow with this system is endless, but ELT suggests using perennials and small vegetables, such as onions, lettuce and radish. They have also had great success with planting herbs, including parsley, basil, rosemary, thyme,

mint, tarragon and chives. To keep the plants healthy, an irrigation system should be set up to supply water from the top of the panel. The water is delivered to the compost by a network of channels at the back of the tray, which also helps excess water to drain away.

Another living wall system is VertiGarden, launched to UK gardeners in 2009. It consists of a steel wall frame that can be attached to a wall with a hook. This holds a polystyrene modular tray, which is first planted up horizontally with herbs, vegetables or bedding plants and then inserted in place. A wire mesh grid on the front of the system prevents plants from falling out.

If you live in a mild climate, a wall panel can be planted with exotics.

Apart from beautifying fairly dull and pedestrian walls, and enabling you to squeeze even more plants into your space, vertical gardens have several other benefits to justify their creation. They are great for the biodiversity of a garden, as the nooks and crannies among the plants provide valuable habitats for insects and other mini-beasts, while the green panels help to reduce home energy consumption. In winter they act like an insulating layer, and in summer the green panels help to cool the property.

Succulents

When I was about ten or eleven years old my parents gave me the responsibility of looking after a plant of *Haworthia attenuata* that had thrived on our sunny kitchen windowsill for many years. I was fascinated by this curious plant, whose untidy rosette of green leaves banded with raised white tubercles reminded me of the waving tentacles of a sea anemone. Despite having to compete for my attention against a Scalextric racing set, Action Man and numerous Corgi cars, the haworthia prospered and grew into a sizeable clump.

The delivery of this plant into my little fingers led to a lifelong fascination with cacti and succulents, and by the time I was in my mid-teens I had already collected several hundred plants that were arranged cheek by jowl on the windowsills of the family house. However, lack of space indoors was a serious threat to my obsession, so I was delighted when, for my sixteenth birthday, I was given a small greenhouse in which to relocate my plants.

For many years I devoted much of my free time to nurturing my colourful little charges, including specimens of *Haworthia*, *Aloe*, *Gasteria*, *Agave*, *Crassula* and *Sedum*, but in my late teens my attention was diverted by a more traditional activity practised by young men: chasing girls. Sadly, my collection suffered (um, that's a white lie—they actually all died) through neglect, but I have always retained an interest in this fascinating group of plants, and have long wished to travel to the warm climes of the Canary Islands to see my favourite group of succulents, aeoniums, growing in the well-drained volcanic soil of Tenerife, Lanzarote, Fuerteventura and Gran Canaria.

Alas, I have yet to visit, but I would like to think that a trip to the Abbey Gardens on Tresco in the Isles of Scilly (an archipelago of 150 islands and rocks) is the next best thing. These subtropical gardens, 25 miles off the coast of Cornwall in the south-west of England, are home to twenty different types of *Aeonium* and make a great showcase to see how these plants can be used in the garden. Apart from the dark and seriously gorgeous *A.* 'Zwartkop' and *A. arboreum* 'Purpureum', which are ubiquitous throughout the gardens, there are many species that defy gravity to make a vertical spectacle. For instance, the arched doorway in the crumbling remains of the old abbey walls is studded with large, green rosettes of *A. cuneatum*, whose mass of coral pink roots, so slender that they resemble the finest filaments, have probed and prodded until becoming firmly embedded between the fissures of the ancient stones. Elsewhere, *A. tabuliforme*, a spectacular plant that forms huge plates of densely overlapping green leaves, grows vertically on walls, appearing as if it has been hung up with picture hooks by the curator of an art gallery.

Opposite: Large walls or fences give garden owners the chance to hang several panels together to completely clothe a vertical surface, as with this planting of *Calibrachoa*. Photograph by VertiGarden.

Drought-tolerant house-leeks spread quickly and are perfect gap fillers.

A short trip by powered launch (motorboat) from Tresco is Saint Mary's, the largest of the Scilly Isles, with a population of just over sixteen hundred. Walking around the island's main town, Hughtown, I was amazed by the rich selection of succulents that thrive without any protection in domestic front gardens. There were huge furcraeas, agaves and crassula, but what really caught my attention were the garden walls that encircle the islanders' properties, many of which are embellished by huge, pendulous clusters of *Aeonium cuneatum*, *A. canariense* and hybrids of these two species. Although some of these may well have spread through self-seeding, most have been given a helping hand by the owner of the house, who will snap off a rosette with a short length of root attached and push it between the rocks of a dry stone wall or into the loose mortar sandwiched between clay bricks. These crude 'cuttings' will quickly anchor themselves and spread slowly to camouflage bare patches of wall.

A combination of low rainfall, humidity from the sea, high light levels, long hours of sunshine and warm winters with very few frosts means that these tender plants thrive in the Isles of Scilly, where the temperature rarely dips below 10°C (50°F). If you are lucky enough to have a garden that enjoys similar conditions you would probably have great success with aeoniums, and even though my London garden doesn't tick all the boxes, aeoniums will even root in the walls here with a little bit of tender loving care.

Before planting it's worth spending a few minutes preparing your wall. You will need a large enough gap to push in your plant and for the roots to spread deeply enough to provide a firm anchor—don't be afraid to use a drill to widen or deepen a gap in the mortar if necessary. Although the climate in the Isles of Scilly means that cuttings will grow easily when stuck into a wall, I like to give mine a helping hand by pushing a good dollop of gritty compost (a loam-based compost is ideal) into the crevice to facilitate rooting. Dampen this slightly with a hand-held sprayer.

In spring or summer take a stem cutting that is 4–6 cm long, or remove a rosette with a short length of stem attached from a parent plant. Remove it carefully with a sharp gardening knife or shears to avoid spoiling the shape of your specimen. Strip any lower leaves away with your fingers and place the cutting on its side for a few days so that a callus forms over the cut end, which will prevent fungal diseases from entering the cut surface. Finally, push your cutting into the vertical side of the wall, inserting the stem firmly into the compost. Roots should form readily.

If your winters are mild and dry, you should be able to leave your plants in place, as the vertical face of the wall should protect its roots from excessive wet. My garden, however, usually suffers from buckets of rain during the bleaker months of the year, along with the occasional frosty day and sometimes snow, so I remove the plant and its plug of compost in late autumn. It might be possible to leave it in situ by protecting it with a simple sheet of horticultural fleece (cover cloth—an American version is available as Reemay) draped over the top, but I've not been brave enough to try this out yet.

Low-growing varieties make the best plants for walls, as the top weight of the large shrubby species will eventually cause the plant to topple out. *Aeonium urbicum*, *A. tabuliforme*, *A. 'Frosty'*, *A. undulatum* subsp. *pseudotabuliforme* (there's a spectacular example at Huntington Gardens in Los Angeles), *A. cuneatum*, *A. lindleyi*, *A. canariense* and *A. sedifolium* are all worth trying, although some are in scarce supply and will need detective work to track down. I really love *A. castello-paivae*, an unusual species with a slightly prostrate habit that makes a mass of wiry stems topped with small rosettes of slender, slate grey leaves ending in a red tip.

An alternative to planting tender succulents is to use *Sempervivum* or *Jovibarba*, which are hardy down to −15°C (5°F). These rosette-forming plants, native to moun-

Most aeoniums are upright, but this plant of *Aeonium castello-paivae* growing in my own garden has a trailing habit.

tainous areas of Europe, are known by amateur gardeners throughout the United Kingdom as houseleeks. Why? Well, it's not because they make a good alternative for leeks when making vichyssoise, but because they were traditionally grown on top of houses to ward off evil spirits and protect from lightning. Where the affiliation to leeks comes from, I don't know, but you would have to have a pretty vivid imagination to ever get this plant mixed up with a root vegetable.

There are many fabulous species and cultivars of *Sempervivum* available, and the *RHS Plant Finder 2007–2008* lists more than a thousand. Their rosettes range in size from a diminutive 5 mm to over 20 cm, and they come in many colours, including shades of grey, green, yellow, red and dark purple, often with a contrasting shade at the tip of each leaf. Some are smothered in fine, cobwebby hairs, while others are a terrific value as they change colour during the year. For instance, *S.* 'Gallivarda' is burgundy in spring, yellowy red in summer, red in early autumn and dark purple a couple of months later. All flower, producing a stout wand holding an explosion of star-shaped pink, purple, red, yellow or cream blooms. However, as sempervivums are monocarpic, the rosette that flowers will die after the colourful spectacle.

To plant in a wall, simply divide a well-established clump by pulling the ro-

Houseleeks thrive on the top of a wall in Devon.

settes apart with your hands, ensuring that each has a length of stem and roots attached. As these have fairly short stems, it's best to plant them in fairly wide and deep gaps to give them a foothold in which to become established. First push some gritty compost into the gap and then insert the rosette. Sempervivums spread quickly and within just a few years you'll have an attractive patch on the wall. However, even though these plants have roots that anchor themselves deeply, the weight of a colony of rosettes, along with flower stalks, can lead to a clump falling. You can help to prevent this by snipping off the occasional rosette to keep the plant within bounds.

For the best-looking wall, choose varieties with small rosettes and avoid large varieties, such as *Sempervivum* 'Othello', which bears a close resemblance to a cabbage. Not only would this look ridiculous growing vertically, but the weight of the rosette would mean you would be forever picking the cutting up off the floor. Among my favourites are *S. montanum* subsp. *montanum*, *S.* 'Atropurpureum', *S.* 'Madeleine' and *S. calcareum* 'Extra', which produces the most geometric rosettes you'll have ever seen, with each tiny green leaf marked at the tip with purple. Perhaps the most perfect for walls, due to its miniature rosettes, is *S. arachnoideum* and the many members of its tribe, all of which are covered in delicate white hair.

Be creative

The main aim of this book is to describe how to make the most of a confined space, but if you don't mind adding to the general clutter of a garden (which I don't, much to the chagrin of my partner and children), it is possible to introduce some decorative features that will enable you to grow even more plants.

In my garden, nestling among the finely cut, glossy leaves of *Geranium palmatum*, which sprawls out beneath a clump of *Phyllostachys nigra*, is a large piece of tufa that I have turned into a container for tender and hardy succulents. This unusual material, bought from an aquatic nursery (although it is also stocked by landscape suppliers), is formed when lime deposits builds up over the years to leave calcium carbonate, a material that is porous, extremely light and very easy to drill, chisel or hack into to make planting pockets.

To make my planter, I drilled holes into the soft stone at random with a large masonry drill bit and then washed the stone by soaking it with a watering can—this removes any dust, grit or dirt. After filling the gaps with a gritty compost mix, I added several rosettes of sempervivum and took stem cuttings from aeoniums, which were stuck into the compost. The stone was then placed in a sunny spot, where the plants continue to thrive. After many years in the garden, the tufa has aged beautifully to boast a wonderful green patina. It's a doddle to look after. If the plants look as if they need it, I'll give them a drink, and other than that, I simply protect the aeoniums by moving the tufa into the greenhouse over winter.

Although succulents look perfect in tufa, you could also try cacti, heathers or alpines such as saxifrages, androsaces, gentians, campanulas and silenes.

In 2004 I came away from the Royal Horticultural Society's Hampton Court Palace Flower Show with more than just tired feet and a bagful of plants. One of the smaller show gardens had lots of novel ideas for planting up interesting objects, and I was fascinated with a brick that had sempervivums growing in it. Back home, I went to my local builders' merchants and scrounged a smooth, red engineering brick (those with three round holes bored into them) to try making a succulent planter myself. There was nothing to it. First fill the holes with gritty compost, then split a sempervivum apart and stick a single rosette into each, ensuring that the roots are firmly embedded in the soil. Finish by watering and putting onto a sunny patio or wherever you want visitors to comment on your unique feature. If the mood takes you, why not try planting up several and arranging them in a pattern, or use them to border a patio, steps or the side of a path.

I was once visiting a friend's garden when I spotted a fabulous old enamel Belfast sink (a shallow version of the more common Butler sink) that was turned on its

Even the most unusual objects can make terrific planters. This kodu, a type of butternut squash spotted at the Coriander Club, a gardening club for Bangladeshi women in London, has been scooped out and turned into a container for an echeveria. Photograph by Benedict Vanheems.

side and almost lost in the undergrowth that prospered down the perimeter of their plot. My excitement at this discovery was lost on everyone, but I convinced the owner that this sink would make a brilliant planter for alpines. Using the sink, he could ensure that these challenging plants were all grown in the ideal compost, and with a bit of manpower (or a sack trolley) the sink could be moved about like a piece of furniture, allowing him to continually change the look of the garden. It would also be perfect for a tiny garden because you could squeeze ten or more plants into a 27 in. by 17 in. space.

If you're not lucky enough to have a sink hidden in the bushes, don't despair. You should be able to buy one from a salvage yard or possibly find one by searching online. A great resource is www.freecycle.org, which operates around the world and is basically a forum for people to give away goods they no longer want.

Planting is easy. First place the sink in its finished position (do it after planting and you risk slipping a few discs) and then plug the drain hole by putting a piece of broken terracotta pot across it. This will allow excess water to drain but will prevent the compost from clogging the hole or spilling out all over the place. Next, fill the sink halfway with a gritty compost mix—I use loam-based compost embellished with some horticultural grit to improve its drainage. Then add the plants while still in their pots, moving them around until you are happy with the display. If you are viewing it from one side, taller plants should be placed at the back with any that have trailing stems placed at the front. If it is to be viewed from all sides, place taller plants in the centre and graduate the height as you work towards the edges.

My alpine sink, pictured just after planting, contains thirteen different plants, including bulbs.

Now decant each alpine from its pot and put it back in position, then fill in the gaps around each with your compost, aiming to leave a gap of about an inch between the surface of the compost and the lip of the sink. To finish, cover the surface with grit. This will leave an attractive finish but will also help to keep the lower leaves of plants dry and prevent rotting. Remove any grit that has fallen into the crowns of plants with a paintbrush, then water the sink gently with a fine rose fitted to a watering can. To add extra interest to the sink you could also insert small pieces of tufa to make a mountainous scene, or arrange lengths of river-worn bog myrtle.

So what should you grow in a sink? There are hundreds of plants you could try, but in my friend's sink I used *Silene uniflora* (syn. *S. maritima*), *Rhodohypoxis baurii*, *Sedum spurium* 'Variegatum', *Sedum spathulifolium* 'Cape Blanco', *Saxifraga* 'Cloth of Gold', *Hereroa glenensis*, *Pratia pedunculata* 'County Park', *Sempervivum* and thrift. In a sink I later planted up in my own garden I have *Arenaria balearica*, *Saxifraga* 'Findling', *Saxifraga paniculata*, *Chaenorhinum origanifolium*, *Silene schafta*, *Silene uniflora*, *Pratia pedunculata*, *Arabis blepharophylla* 'Spring Charm', *Campanula poscharskyana*, *Pritzelago alpina* and *Armeria juniperifolia* 'Bevan's Variety'. It has been underplanted with bulbs of *Iris* 'Harmony' (Reticulata) and *Iris danfordiae*.

Looking after a sink is a breeze. Dead-head flowers, remove tatty foliage and provide some protection from winter rain—a simple way is to pile up some bricks on either side of the sink and then lay a sheet of rigid plastic over the top, which will protect the plants from excessive moisture while allowing them to breathe.

There are several other ways of growing different groups of plants that need specific conditions. In most small gardens there isn't enough room to build a pond, but you could try growing aquatic plants in a half wooden barrel (see chapter 4 for more on this).

Carnivorous plants have a reputation for being temperamental, and there's no point pretending otherwise. They are like a high-maintenance lover who never tires in making unreasonable demands on your time, energy and attention. I have to admit that this 'treat 'em mean, keep 'em keen' approach works, because once you have spent time with any members of this fascinating group of plants, you'll be their faithful horticultural servant.

I grow mine in a 12 in. pot that has been filled with carnivorous-plant compost, essentially pure peat with added grit for drainage. It is home to a Venus flytrap (*Dionaea muscipula*), a sundew (*Drosera capensis*) and two types of pitcher plants: *Sarracenia purpurea*, a short, stocky species with purple-veined pitchers and *S.* 'Stevensii', a taller plant with white-splashed pitchers. Thanks to breeding work, many different plants are now available, and it's worth tracking down a good supplier, as your average garden centre will only stock a limited range.

For healthy plants, keep the compost moist at all times using rain water (tap water is fine in an emergency). You can ensure the compost never dries out by placing a tray or large saucer under the pot, topping it up whenever it runs dry. Pandering to these plants' requirements will ensure they thrive. Recently my reward was to see a Venus flytrap flower for the first time—its delicate flower spike held tiny white blooms.

If you live in a warm climate, where some of these plants originate, the container can probably be left outdoors all year round, but in the United Kingdom it is advisable to put the pot in a frost-free place over winter. Many sarracenia will survive temperatures down to −5°C (23°F), but sundew is frost tender, and Venus flytraps, which herald from North Carolina and South Carolina, are unlikely to make it through winter if temperatures reach 0°C (32°F).

It's possible to grow lots of plants even if you have a room in a high-rise flat. Yes, I am being serious. The Victorians were huge fans of terrariums or bottle gardens, which is a fun way to grow houseplants or plants that need high humidity in a

Feed me! Curious carnivorous plants will thrive in a big pot as long as the compost is kept permanently moist.

really compact space. Growing in bottles, fishbowls, empty aquariums or large carboys (glass storage jars) reached its peak in the 1970s, until this technique became as passé as macramé plant pot holders, black forest gateau and knitted toilet roll covers. Well, I'm going to stick my head on the line and suggest that it's time for them to make a comeback—they are an ideal way for flat dwellers to add some greenery to their high-rise homes.

You can use whatever glass container you fancy, but I have a bottle garden made from a large Kilner storage jar that sits on my kitchen windowsill. Prepare your jar using the following recipe. First add a layer of expanded clay pebbles for drainage, then cover with some powdered charcoal to keep the compost fresh and smelling nice (I got mine from a pet shop). Finish by pouring in some multi-purpose compost until about a quarter full. To plant, use a long-handled spoon to excavate some holes and then lower plants in and firm into place with the back of the spoon.

Fill your jar with foliage plants rather than those that flower, choosing either plants that are naturally small or buying plugs of those that will grow tall over time. Any of these would be ideal: *Ficus pumila* (creeping fig), *Chamaedorea elegans* (parlour palm), *Maranta leuconeura* var. *erythroneura* (prayer plant), *Hypoestes phyllostachya* (polka dot plant), *Dracaena sanderiana* (ribbon plant), *Plectranthus verticillatus*, *Selaginella kraussiana* 'Aurea', *Adiantum raddianum* (maidenhair fern) and *Iresine herbstii* (bloodleaf).

After planting, water well and then close the lid of the jar to increase the humidity and reduce the need for regular watering. If the inside of the jar clouds over, simply open the lid for a few seconds until it clears.

Maintenance is easy. Trim any plants that try to escape the confines of the jar, and water whenever the compost appears to be drying out. In time, plants will crowd each other out and need replanting.

Super-fast colour

Hardy annuals are like the Indianapolis 500 or Formula 1 racing champions of the plant world—sow their seeds in spring and they'll accelerate into life. In just a few weeks you'll have a splash of colour that will last throughout the summer and may continue to provide a spectacle until the middle of autumn.

The only other group of plants that can provide such a dazzling array of shades so quickly is the half-hardy annuals, such as petunias, busy Lizzies (impatiens) and African marigolds, but although these flowers are loved by many and can be useful in the garden, most are too brash for my taste. More often than not, when they are planted in the garden (even by skilled hands) they come perilously close to resembling a municipal bedding display. Yuck.

Hardy annuals are ideal to plug bare patches in a bed or border, possibly in a space that you never got round to filling with a new perennial or shrub. The flowers can be enjoyed throughout the summer, giving you plenty of time to decide what permanent plant to grow in the gap. They can also be sown under shrubs, to provide a skirt of colour to hide naked stems, or grown in crevices between slabs or stones that make up a patio or path. I've never done it, but it may be worth trying to sow seeds in a large container that houses a specimen tree or fruit plant.

Growing hardy annuals is a breeze. First you need to prepare the soil. Hoe off any weeds in the gap you want to fill, then fork the site over, improving the soil with plenty of garden compost or leaf mould. To get the plants off to a great start, scatter some granules of a balanced fertilizer over the soil, following the instructions on the packet, and mix into the surface with a rake. Aim to leave a stone-free, level surface. If you can, try to prepare the soil several weeks before sowing.

You can raise plants in seed trays or in nursery beds, but it's quicker, easier and far less finicky to sow seeds directly into the soil. To do this, mark out where you want to sow the seeds, using a cane to score the ground or by trickling sand through your hands to create a planting pattern. Then, using a cane or the back of a rake, make shallow drills within the area to be planted. Seeds should then be sown thinly in the trenches, covered over and watered gently using a watering can fitted with a fine rose.

In some circumstances it may not be possible to prepare the ground properly, possibly due to lack of room between plants in a bed or because you don't want to damage the roots of other plants. In such situations prepare the soil as best you can, trying to at least loosen the soil with a fork (pitchfork) and leaving a crumbly surface. Then broadcast the seed and ensure it has good contact with the soil by raking it into the surface.

Keep the plants well watered while they are establishing and thin out rows to allow plants to develop fully. If you do this carefully, using a hand fork to pull the plant from the ground, you can replant them into gaps elsewhere in the garden. Taller-growing varieties will need staking to prevent them from flopping in heavy rain or being flattened by a gust of wind. You can do this by cutting twiggy sticks from a bushy shrub or tree and pushing them among the plants when they are about 3 in. high.

That's it. Enjoy the show, and either remove plants before they set seed or let them self-sow for another great display next year.

I love to sit with a selection of plant catalogues making long lists of the plants I want to grow and then editing my selection to a more reasonable handful. It's easy to get carried away when ordering hardy annuals as there are hundreds of good varieties, but choose prudently. Select plants that will suit the style of your garden or that will work well with the neighbouring plants, along with being the right height, colour and shape for the area you want to fill.

California poppies are an essential hardy annual with blooms that last from early summer into the middle of autumn. They come in a vast palette of colours and generally reach 9 in. (23 cm). *Eschscholzia californica* 'Golden Tears' has burnt yellow flowers, *E. californica* 'Golden Values' is yellow with a rich orange centre and *E. californica* 'Sun Shades' has bright orange blooms. For scarlet flowers, try *E. californica* 'Red Chief', or for something more muted, *E. californica* 'Ivory Castle', whose flowers are white with bright yellow stamens. If you like a poppy with more unusual looks, go for *E. californica* 'Apricot Chiffon'—its apricot petals are enticingly wavy.

Another large tribe worth checking out is *Nigella*, or love-in-a-mist, which has ferny foliage and bright flowers that are followed by lantern-like seedpods. *Nigella damascena* 'Miss Jekyll' has light blue flowers and *N. papillosa* 'Midnight' dark purple blooms. My favourite is the extraordinary *N. papillosa* 'African Bride', which has blooms the shape of a court jester's hat. Growing to 24 in. (60 cm), the snowy white petals sit beneath a prominent, heart-shaped blade that terminates with a cluster of almost black stamens that curve downwards.

Cerinthe major 'Purpurascens' (honeywort) is a tall plant, growing up to 30 in. (75 cm), with glaucous foliage, purple bracts and blue flowers. *Cerinthe minor* 'Bouquet Gold' looks completely different—much more compact, reaching 18 in. (45 cm), with golden flowers perched above mounds of green leaves that are heavily spotted white.

You can also grow several annual grasses. *Briza maxima* (big quaking grass) has slender stems topped by pendulous flowers and grows to 18 in. (45 cm). *Lagurus ovatus* (hare's tail) has plump, fluffy white seed heads that my children love to stroke.

Lovers of dark flowers should try *Centaurea cyanus* 'Black Ball' for its crimson pompom blooms. *Limnanthes douglasii* is another good option, a vibrant plant with yellow flowers with a white tip on each petal. A native to California, where it is known as meadow foam, *L. douglasii* has the amusing common name of scrambled egg plant in the United Kingdom. It is a magnet to bees. If you want an unusual flower, you can't go far wrong with *Bupleurum rotundifolium* 'Green Gold'. It grows to 24 in. (60 cm) and has eucalyptus-like foliage and star-shaped, yellow flowers.

Shady customers

When we moved into our terraced house, the garden we inherited was miserable, but within a couple of weeks I had a blank canvas. I started to add the structural bones of my new garden (path, raised bed, greenhouse and deck), followed by the

Side passages can be tricky to plant up, but a pergola above this generous passage has transformed the space into a sanctuary for shade-loving plants.
Photograph by Jonathan Buckley, courtesy of The Garden Collection.

sun-loving plants that would bask in the south-facing plot. All of these sun worshippers thrived, but in planting the garden I had created pockets of shade behind larger plants or in the shadow of structures such as my greenhouse.

Although there may be a tendency to curse gloomy spots like these, especially when you have a sun trap, I looked upon it as an opportunity to grow some of my favourite shade-loving plants. Many of these are planted in an 18 in. by 20 in. (45 cm by 50 cm) rectangular patch between my brick storage seat and fence, which I rather pompously call my shade bed. In late winter, interest is provided by a clump of *Asarum splendens*, an evergreen perennial that spreads slowly and has glossy, kidney-shaped green leaves that are heavily speckled silver. Growing only to about 4 in. (10 cm), this native of the United States, where it's commonly known as wild ginger, has foliage that conceals masses of stumpy, mucky brown, pitcher-like flowers that are heavily veined purple.

Close by is a pink-flowered form (it also comes in white) of *Begonia grandis* subsp. *evansiana*, a wonderful tuberous perennial that heralds from China and Malaysia. Growing to 20 in. (50 cm), it has heart-shaped green leaves with orangey undersides that look stunning when backlit by the sun. In late summer its stems carry pendulous pink flowers above the leaves, while the leaf axils hold tiny bulbils—in its native environment these would root when they fall to the floor, but in the United Kingdom they are generally killed by the frost. This begonia can withstand temperatures down to 0°C (32°F), when it will retreat underground before emerging again in spring.

Rubbing shoulders with *Begonia grandis* subsp. *evansiana* is *B. palmata*. Slightly shorter at 12 in. (30 cm), this hardy (to about −9°C) Chinese species has spread to make a big clump and has large, lobed leaves carried on succulent stems and pink flowers that appear in early summer. I love to watch its showy leaves slowly unfurl from the ground in spring. It's magical.

Late-season colour in the shade bed comes courtesy of *Saxifraga* 'Cotton Crochet', which has made a tidy clump of neatly scalloped dark green leaves. In late autumn and early winter, sprays of spidery white flowers perch 12 in. (30 cm) above the clumps. It is a delicate and beautiful plant that really deserves to be known more.

There are several shady spots in a bed on the east-facing side of my garden. Against the fence I have planted ×*Fatshedera lizei* (tree ivy), a wall shrub whose leaves are so glossy they look like they've been individually polished by hand. This plant has grown quickly to cover almost an entire 6 ft. by 6 ft. (1.8 m by 1.8 m) panel and has been trained against wires that fan out from a central point at the bottom of the fence. It really is a good value plant, providing verdant colour all year round and umbels of white flowers in autumn. It is also fairly well behaved, allowing me to keep it tightly restrained against the fence with twine—this is most important as I

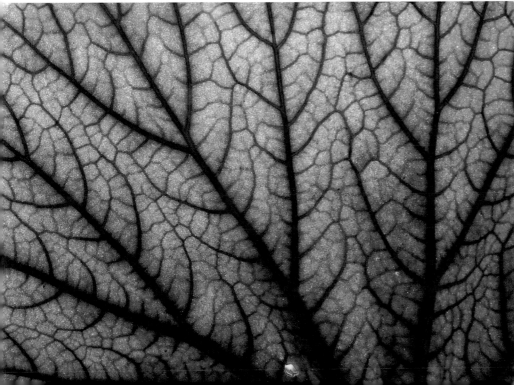

Hardy *Begonia palmata* and *B. grandis* subsp. *evansiana* rub shoulders at the side of my raised brick storage seat.

The effect of light shining through *Begonia grandis* subsp. *evansiana* is stunning.

don't have enough space to grow a shrub or climber that would billow out too much, stealing valuable bed space.

Much of the shade in this bed is the result of two big clumps of black bamboo (*Phyllostachys nigra*). Immediately beneath them I have planted a trio of plants from County Park Nursery in Essex, which has an eclectic mix of plants from New Zealand, Australia and Tasmania, including many that were found on plant hunting expeditions by the nursery's owner, Graham Hutchins. *Pseudopanax lessonii* grows well in a spot in really dense shade and is a spreading shrub with branches carrying open, palmate leaves that are green and glossy. If there was a bit more light I would have preferred to grow the showier *P. lessonii* 'Gold Splash', an attractive variegated shrub, whose green leaves are heavily marked yellow. In a site that receives slightly more light I have planted *Corokia* ×*virgata* 'Sunsplash', a variegated shrub with wiry stems clothed with oval leaves splashed with cream, yellow and green. In an open spot it would reach 10 in. (25 cm) tall with a similar spread, but the cramped nature of my bed helps to restrict its growth. In between the pseudopanax and corokia is *Macropiper excelsum*, a very unusual shrub from New Zealand that is known by the indigenous Maori people as *kawakawa*, a reference to the bitter taste of its leaves—in fact every part of the plant is used by the Maori, from the roots to the flowers. Unfortunately the plant isn't blessed in the looks department—it makes a large shrub, up to 13 ft. (4 m) in perfect conditions, and has roundish green leaves. I have to admit that I bought it solely because it doesn't mind semi-shade and had an interesting story to tell.

Not all of the shade-loving plants I have bought have done so well. On a visit to Crûg Farm Nursery near Caernarfon in Wales, I fell in love with *Impatiens omeiana* and snapped up a specimen to grow in my London garden. Related to the humble busy Lizzy, this species is native to China and makes a 12 in. (30 cm) tall clump of red-stemmed branches clothed with slender 3 in. (8 cm) leaves with a yellowish mid-rib and veins. I planted it under *Cercis canadensis* 'Forest Pansy' and it did very well for a season, thriving in the damp, shady spot. However, due to drought, a hose pipe ban was imposed on the south-east of England during 2006 and getting enough water to the plants in the garden became difficult during a long, hot, dry summer. Eventually it went up to the great plant heaven in the sky. A group of three *Lysimachia minoricensis* met a similar fate. This beautiful foliage perennial grows to 17 in. (43 cm) and has big green leaves that are delicately marked with silver. The foliage is remarkably similar in shape to that of a hosta, and I discovered that it, too, is irresistible to slugs. Within a few days my handsome plants had been reduced to pathetic stumps that stood just proud of the soil.

An alternative to using permanent plants to fill shady spots is to treat the garden like a stage set and dress it with houseplants or tender plants grown in pots—

either place pots into position on the surface or plunge them into the soil. This way you can change the display several times a year and even use sun-loving plants, which can be moved whenever they start to sulk. I have seen several displays that have worked well. In one garden, the owner created an exotic look in a shady space by using *Lantana*, *Protea*, Swiss cheese plant (*Monstera deliciosa*) and funky-leaved *Begonia rex*. The plants are changed after they flower or show signs of being unhappy in the shade, and everything is hoicked from the soil in autumn and put into a frost-free place over winter. The same gardener also placed mirrors at the base of his front garden wall. This reflected more light into the compact space dominated by the dense planting scheme and could also be considered a trompe-l'oeil, a visual trick used by garden designers to make you think the garden is actually larger than it is. However, as the mirrors are at ankle height, I'd imagine that only cats, ants or worms could possibly be taken in by this deceptive device.

2
Going Up

AS SOON AS YOU have filled every inch of soil with plants, and have found the perfect plants to grow against your walls and fences, you can turn your attention to all of the vertical spaces so often left bare because they are not considered suitable for plants.

How far from reality this point of view is. The vertical surface of low-level garden walls, flat roofs, drainpipes, the doorframes of greenhouses and the sides of sheds can all support plants. Most of the time this is worth doing because it allows you to squeeze more plants into your garden for the sake of, well, growing more plants, but you might also want to grow plants against a vertical structure to hide it. An outdoor storage area where you stash your bicycles, or an ugly sweep of metal railings that separates your property from your neighbour's, can be softened with plants. For instance, a fast-growing climber could be trained over the storage shed, while the railings could be masked with a series of troughs attached to brackets—fill them with seasonal flowers or trailing foliage plants and you won't notice the harsh boundary behind them.

Another way to boost vertical interest in the garden is to make trees and shrubs work extra hard for their keep. A bare trunk makes the ideal support for an annual climber. Since the plant will only rely on the tree's network of branches for a season, it will never suffocate its host, and using annual climbers will help to keep the show interesting as you can change the display every year.

The branches of trees or a stubborn old stump that refuses to be hoisted from the ground, or which you want to keep because its gnarled branches add sculptural

Opposite: If there's no room to spread out, there's only one way to go—up. The pillars of this faux ruin make the perfect supports for a passion flower. Photograph by Steven Wooster, courtesy of The Garden Collection.

Ugly metal railings can be disguised by planting troughs filled with annual flowers.

interest to the garden, are perfect for supporting plants that grow on trees in their native environment.

For instance, such a spot could become home to a collection of brightly coloured bromeliads. If the tree is dead or mature, you could attach a plastic pot to it with tacks or nails, and then slide the bromeliad's small pot into the slightly larger one. Position the plant carefully, inside the fork of the tree or behind a branch, to ensure that its pot remains hidden from view. If you can, position the pot at a slight angle so that the rosette of leaves and showy flowers can be seen clearly. Avoid putting nails into young trees. Instead remove plants from their containers, wrap in hessian (burlap) and tie to the branches of the tree.

Whatever vertical surfaces you have, whether or not I've mentioned them here, consider planting them up. The amount of colour and extra plants you can shoehorn in is something you'll only ever take delight in and will never live to regret.

Greenhouses

I can't imagine gardening without a greenhouse. It's essential for overwintering plants, storing materials and raising plants from cuttings, but boy is mine ugly. The aluminium frame lacks the beauty of a cedar model, and it has none of the grace of those faux Georgian-style structures often found in glossy gardening magazine advertisements. Aesthetically it is displeasing for most of the year, but it really comes into its own from late spring when I daub the entire exterior with a coat of white shade paint. It becomes a glowing white carbuncle and nobody has ever been heard to say, 'Ooh, isn't it pretty'. If I had time and patience I could lessen the effect by securing sheets of green shade netting to the interior instead, but unfortunately I have neither in abundance, so I'll stick to a paint job that takes five minutes.

Plants arranged neatly on the interior shelves and staging partially help to

Pick your greenhouse carefully, as some models will dominate a small space. This is the smallest I could find that I could still squeeze inside.

perk up the structure—this display changes often but generally consists of succulents, pelargoniums, tender fuchsias and any other plants that I don't have room for in the garden—but I have been attempting to make the whole thing look more interesting by growing plants around the frame of the door.

Before I first started planting anything in the greenhouse, I needed to find a way to support the plants. This was easy. I used the existing grooves in the frame and fitted them with clips that I normally use to hold bubble wrapping for winter insulation. These were then used as a guide for a length of plastic-coated gardening wire, which was wrapped around the clips and pulled fairly taut.

As the greenhouse is protected from the vagaries of the weather and heated over winter, I decided to grow tender climbers. The first plant I tried out was *Lophospermum* 'Red Dragon' (syn. *Maurandya* 'Red Dragon'), which was given to me by Ray Brown of Plant World Seeds in Devon. His nursery is full of the most amazing plants, and when I spotted this climber he suggested I try it. It's a gorgeous, fast-growing plant with long, red trumpet flowers, and it did well clambering up the wire and being held in place with twine as it grew. Unfortunately, my love affair with this choice plant was short lived, as it rotted due to the compost becoming extremely damp over winter. Despite this, I can thoroughly recommend it, and Ray has several other varieties that can be grown from seed. *Maurandya* 'Bridal Bouquet' has large white flowers that are more flared than 'Red Dragon', while M. *barclayana* has cobalt blue blooms.

The job of replacing the lophospermum went to *Jasminum polyanthum*. I had bought the plant as a Valentine's Day gift for my partner, but her lack of green fingers meant the plant was teetering somewhere between life and death. Rather than see it suffer any longer I decided to rescue it from the house and grow it in the greenhouse. Planted in a large container, it grows vigorously up its supports, flowering prolifically from late summer until winter. Despite being tiny, these small white blooms are packed with perfume, and en masse the scent is intoxicating. As long as it doesn't dry out and the temperature doesn't fall below 0°C (32°F), you shouldn't have any problems with it.

Hanging baskets

Some of the horticultural cognoscenti turn up their noses at hanging baskets, considering them garish containers of bad taste. I suppose they have a point. In the wrong hands a hanging basket is often filled with an assortment of brightly coloured, clashing tender annuals and hung in a prominent position from the walls of a house so that everyone walking past has the opportunity to marvel at it. I consider

this to be the gardening equivalent of a businessman wearing dayglo socks or a 'novelty' tie under a sober suit: it's not sophisticated, wacky or attractive, and not in the slightest bit amusing.

But in the right pair of hands, and used sparingly (the practice of covering every bare bit of wall, as demonstrated by many pubs over summer, should be avoided as this is the floral version of pebble dashing), a hanging basket can embellish a home or other sterile vertical surface such as a fence or garden wall. They can even be used to add some extra interest to the boughs of trees or, if mounted on a pole, to break up the monotony of a bed or border.

When you don't have a traditional garden, walls and windowsills can be utilized by hanging baskets and window troughs.

I only have two baskets. One is at the back of the house, the other to the side of the door in my north-facing, shady front garden. The garden here is tiny, but I've still managed to squeeze loads of plants in, including *Acanthus mollis* 'Hollard's Gold' , *Epimedium ×youngianum* 'Niveum', *Luzula sylvatica* 'Aurea', *Brunnera macrophylla* 'Betty Bowring', *Maianthemum racemosum*, *Dicentra spectabilis* 'Alba' and several ferns, including *Polystichum setiferum* Congestum Group. The choice of plants gives the space a leafy feel, punctuated by splashes of yellow and white. To marry in with this theme I've made a hanging basket that consists entirely of spider plants (*Chlorophytum*).

Whenever I see spider plants indoors, I'm transported back to my childhood in the 1970s, when no room was complete without a dusty specimen growing limply in a macramé basket. However, outdoors they are resplendent. Free from the restraints of a tiny pot and relishing the fresh air and improved levels of light, they are extremely perky and the strappy leaves are an emerald green rather than a deathly shade of grey. Within an instant, this basket provides a cool, lush feel to this partially shaded spot.

Although the common variegated spider plant, *Chlorophytum comosum* 'Variegatum', looks great, other cultivars of this species are also worth trying. 'Vittatum' has white leaves edged with green, 'Golden Glow' has emerald green leaves with a

Spider plants (*Chlorophytum*) give my shady front door an exotic facelift.

central golden stripe and 'Aureomarginata' has leaves with yellow edges. If you don't want anything flashy, just pick the straight species, which is green.

I grow mine in a basket 35–45 cm in diameter with a liner of sisal hemp, although wool, coconut fibre or anything else that looks natural would do. There are two layers, with plants offset from each other, and three plants placed in the top. After all danger of frost has passed, I hang it from a bracket on the wall. Plants grow incredibly quickly, and before long I have lots of wiry stems carrying baby plants. If you live in a temperate climate, it's best to move the basket to a frost-free place over winter, as spider plants can't tolerate much below 7°C (45°F).

Houseplants can be used for sunnier spots. Trailing cactus, such as *Rhipsalis*, *Zygocactus* and *Rhipsalidopsis*, are perfect, or you could try *Sedum morganianum*, sometimes known as donkey's tail. If you have a very warm, protected position you could get away with growing monkey cups (*Nepenthes* spp.), a tender carnivorous plant that I only dare grow in my greenhouse.

Among the best houseplants to grow in baskets are the trailing tradescantias, or spiderworts. This large tribe of perennials from North, Central and South America are instantly recognizable for their fleshy stems clothed with oval, slightly pointed leaves. My favourites include *Tradescantia pallida* 'Purpurea', which has dark purple leaves that are slightly hairy—in the United States there's a fantastic pink and purple variegated variety that I'm itching to grow (you might see it offered under *Setcreasea pallida* 'Variegata'). Another eyecatching spiderwort is *T. zebrina*, originating from Mexico, which has dark green edges and a green stripe between two bands of silver. Like all spiderworts, it grows fast and is extremely easy to propagate.

In my back garden, the hanging basket display changes during the year, depending on the plants I find in my local garden centre. For instance, in spring I might have a subtle medley of yellow and pastel pink violas, trailing variegated ivy and dwarf narcissus, and then throw in *Carex buchananii* to give the display some extra texture. When the show starts to fade, usually in mid-May, I might plant the basket with a sole *Begonia boliviensis* 'Bonfire', a pendulous variety with elongated triangular leaves and the most amazing orangey red flowers. It's a fantastic variety that has much going for it—it's easy to grow, flowers for months and is an instant attention grabber. Everybody wants to grow it when they see it in full flight.

To paraphrase George H W Bush, I do not like trailing petunias. And I haven't liked them since I was a little kid. And to that you can add many other 'traditional' bedding plants. Even when I was a young gardener they were a turn-off to me, and I could never understand why, during late spring, usually sedate garden centres became noisy and chaotic as these plants first became available. The scenes I have witnessed in garden centres or nurseries at this time of year remind me of the New Year's sale at Harrods, with people pushing, shoving and racing around to get what they want before anyone else snaps it up. If you dare venture into your local plant emporium at this time of the year, expect to witness the occasional flare-up of temper or to see a couple of customers lose their dignity as they wrestle over the last cell pack of pink busy Lizzies.

Although I'll give most flowering bedding plants the cold shoulder, I do like some of the foliage plants that are displayed alongside them. These are usually sold as trailing plants to be mixed with half-hardy annuals in baskets. Among the best is *Dichondra argentea* 'Silver Falls', which produces a mass of long stems clothed with tiny silver leaves. *Dichondra micrantha* 'Emerald Falls' is less of a head turner, but its pure green foliage provides a lush, cool look.

Most morning glories are grown for their showy flowers, but the cultivars of *Ipomoea batatas* (sweet potato) are perfect for a jungly look and are grown for their attractive leaves—in fact the flowers are almost insignificant. 'Blackie' has dark, lobed leaves, while 'Margarita' has acid green foliage. If you're brave you could even try 'Pink Frost', sometimes called 'Variegata', which has green leaves splashed with pink and white. The fleshy pink tubers are edible, although those who have tried them say they are not as tasty as commercial varieties of sweet potato (or yam). Alas, I've yet to cook up a storm with mine, so I can't say whether they have a secondary use as a vegetable.

The fiery red flowers of *Begonia boliviensis* 'Bonfire' cascade from this hanging basket from early summer until October.

Many other foliage plants look good in baskets. Closely allied to the family of invasive weeds, *Oxalis* 'Burgundy Wine' is far better behaved and makes a neat hummock of foliage. It has trifoliate, dark purple leaves that make the ideal backdrop for its pure white flowers, which appear in spring and summer. 'Black Velvet' is even darker, while 'Frosted Jade' has lime green leaves. All die back in autumn but will bounce back into life in spring as long as they are given some protection from the worst of the winter weather.

I'm very taken by the single-coloured and variegated trailing forms of *Plectranthus* and have several that were grown from cuttings and given to me by plant-loving friends. They are great in baskets and are sometimes grouped together under the common name of Swedish ivy, which refers to their use as a houseplant in Scandinavia. Perfect in hanging baskets outdoors over summer, they will need some protection over winter if temperatures in your area dip beneath 5°C (41°F). The trailing purplish stems of *P. madagascariensis* 'Variegated Mintleaf' are clothed with lots of variegated, toothed leaves that are green with irregular white edges—if happy, the pendulous stems can grow to 10 ft. (3 m). The rich, golden foliage of *P. ciliatus* 'Easy Gold' is marked with splashes of dark green and perfect for lighting up a gloomy spot.

Hanging baskets can be used to allow you to squeeze more edible plants into your garden. Tumbling tomatoes are the obvious crop to grow and will do much

Purple oxalis looks good in a lighter-coloured hanging basket.

In mild climates, Swedish ivy (*Plectranthus*) can be grown outside all year round, but it needs protecting where frosts are common.

better when raised up a tad. When tomatoes are grown in pots on a patio or deck, their spreading stems take up a lot of floor space, and you will probably find yourself squishing the odd fruit underfoot as you walk past it. Placing them low also leaves them vulnerable to being eaten or fouled on by pets or wild creatures. Planting a tomato up high allows it to grow unhindered and makes picking a lot easier. Choosing what to grow is a pleasure as there are so many, including yellow, red and orange varieties. My current favourite is 'Hundreds and Thousands', a prolific cropper with marble-sized fruit (the breeder claims that each plant can produce a staggering two thousand in a season)—unfortunately, my children love to graze on the fruit *d'jardin*, so most of these never make it into the kitchen. (If 'Hundreds and Thousands' is unavailable in your area, you might try the comparable 'Red Grape'.) Dwarf French beans, especially the more ornamental varieties with yellow or purple pods, and alpine strawberries will also do well in baskets.

Although hanging baskets are traditionally hung from the walls of a house, I saw an interesting technique used in a small town garden that might be worth experimenting with. To give a border more vertical interest, the owner had sunk a pole into the middle of a bed and then mounted a hanging basket on top. Crocus, muscari and dwarf narcissus were planted for spring, while bedding plants were elbowed in to give a splash of summer colour. The choice of plants didn't appeal to me at all,

Pendulous varieties of fruit, such as tomato 'Hundreds and Thousands', are ideal for hanging baskets.

but I thought this was a clever way of making use of dead space, and I could imagine it working well in my own garden, planted with a solitary trailing foliage plant.

But, I hear you ask, what kind of hanging baskets should we choose for our tasteful trailers? I don't like plastic-coated wire, and taste forbids me from recommending anything made out of plastic, unless you can completely hide its unglamorous surfaces by planting around the sides as well. If your idea is to only put plants in the top of the basket, go for natural rattan, which looks good with just about everything, or a gorgeous, Victorian-style cast-iron basket. (If you choose cast-iron, make sure you've screwed the bracket securely to the wall or you'll wake up to a miserable sight one morning—the weight of the container will drag it from the wall and your display will end up as a pile of compost mixed up with bits of broken plant.)

Pick your hanging basket carefully. Decorative iron containers provide a stylish, touch, but you need to ensure that brackets are fixed firmly to the wall to hold the weight.

The front porch

The part of East London where I live is dominated by street upon street of nine-teenth-century terraced houses with a protruding bay window at the front. Sadly, many of these windows were converted during the 1970s and 1980s by ill-advised homeowners and property developers who thought period homes should be given a modern facelift. What a crime. Close by are many homes where the old wooden sash windows have been replaced with uPVC (vinyl) and heritage features such as decorative columns, bosses (decorative stonework mouldings) and deep stone win-dowsills have been removed. In many cases the sloping slate tile roofs above the bay windows have been replaced with a flat roof clad with roofing felt.

While the original look of the house may have been erased forever, you have to look at the positives, and the flat roof that remains is the perfect place to grow plants in pots.

An area like this can be transformed by arranging lots of plants together, and the more creative you are, the better it will look. I once worked at a horticultural college and was responsible for installing temporary plant displays for meetings, college stage productions and the like by putting bedding plants and houseplants together and arranging them until I was happy with the look. I'd start off at the back with taller plants or raise interesting plants up on pots so that I could graduate the height. I would then work forward, making sure the display was well balanced and that any plastic pots at the front were hidden—spider plants (*Chlorophytum*) are excellent for masking the edges of pots.

I've seen a great display above a bay window where a similar approach has been taken. After ensuring that the roof was entirely waterproof, by adding a thick layer of bitumen over the top of the existing covering, the owner built a display that adds year-round interest. Early in the year it features pansies, fuchsias and *Oxalis*, followed by green and white zantedeschias, begonias, geraniums and purple aeoniums. In summer the centrepiece, raised up so it can be seen very well at the back, is a pale pink brugmansia.

A flat roof above the front door or any other part of the house could be transformed in the same way. A word of caution: before rushing out to get the ladder and adding lots of plants, first check that the structure is not decrepit and will be able to take the weight of the containers. Another must is to work out how you are going to water the plants. Climbing a ladder with a watering can every day is a chore, and you might even forget to do it. Save yourself time by installing an automatic irrigation system, making sure the network of tubes is hidden as discreetly as possible.

Using climbers on other plants

I've visited many large gardens where the owners have planted a rambling rose or clematis at the foot of a tree and trained it into the branches to give a lofty burst of colour. It's a good idea—the trees often blossom in spring, and it's a long wait for autumn fruit, so this trick ensures that trees earns their keep in between by becoming hosts for summer-flowering plants.

Although I don't have a tree that could support a rampant rose or clematis, I do have plants that can easily bear the weight of an annual climber, such as *Cercis canadensis* 'Forest Pansy' and some hardy bananas, *Musa basjoo*.

Among my favourite annual climbers are the morning glories. They come in such a wide range of colours, many with attractive foliage, and I find them completely irresistible—whenever I browse a seed catalogue I feel like a child in a sweet shop and tend to order more varieties than I'll ever get round to sowing.

Perhaps my all-time favourite, both for its evocative name and its saucer-sized white blooms, is the moonflower, *Ipomoea alba*, which lifts the garden at dusk with its heady scent. Unfortunately, it's too vigorous to grow into my small trees, but I thought I'd mention it anyway—it's a splendid plant, and if you have room for a large pot, I suggest trying to grow it up a wigwam of canes.

Better for training into small plants are smaller-flowered morning glories. Most are instantly recognizable, with large, saucer-shaped flowers and oval leaves, but some are decidedly different. Take, for instance, *Ipomoea quamoclit* 'Cardinal Climber'. It is a smasher, with exciting ferny foliage that looks so different from any others, and makes a lovely backdrop to a mass of opulent scarlet flowers. *Ipomoea lobata*, sometimes sold as *Mina lobata*, is another morning glory that stands out from the rest. Rather than having trumpet-shaped flowers, it boasts arching stems clad with rows of tubular flowers that change from red to orange to lemon as they age. If you need an easy-to-grow annual climber to provide an exotic look to your space, this is the plant to go for.

The best-known morning glory, in the United Kingdom at least, is *Ipomoea tricolor* 'Heavenly Blue'. It's such a reliable plant, and although most gardeners know it well, it will still turn heads with its large, sky blue flowers. For something a bit darker, try *I. purpurea* 'Grandpa Otts', whose violet-blue flowers almost seem to glow, each marked with a red star. Or for lighter-coloured flowers, go for *I. purpurea* 'Caprice', which has pale pink blooms with darker pink markings. It would look lovely grown into a plant clothed with dark foliage.

Morning glories are almost foolproof. I start them off in April, sowing seeds into Jiffy-7s (a dried compost pellet, enclosed by thin netting, which expands when soaked in water), and then put them in a heated propagator until they germinate. Roots appear fairly quickly through the sides of the netting, so I then move them into a small pot and re-pot them regularly until they are ready to go outdoors in late May. There's no trick to planting them—just give them as much sun as possible. When the plants are finally stopped in their tracks by frost, all you have to do is dig them up and put the debris on the compost heap.

Although much of my inspiration has come from visiting other gardens or seeing how plants grow in the wild, I have also picked up ideas in some unusual places. Among them is Cotswold Wildlife Park in rural Oxfordshire, where head gardener Tim Miles creates the most stunning temporary, exotic displays with tender plants. In the walled garden, home to meerkats, otters and many brightly coloured birds that caw and call noisily throughout the day, are palm trees whose naked trunks are sometimes transformed by the presence of climbing plants that would turn to mush at the mere mention of the word frost. On one visit, Tim had plunged a pot of a jazzy bougainvillea into the ground next to a palm tree and tied its stems to the hairy trunk, simply by spreading the stems around its circumference and securing them with loops of subtle green twine. If you try this in your own garden, you can leave the vine in place until mid-autumn if you live in a mild climate (bougainvillea need to be kept about 2°C [36°F] or the leaves will drop off), but you'll need to bring it indoors as the weather starts to cool.

I'm not sure what variety of bougainvillea Tim used at the wildlife park, but there are many fabulous plants available in many colours. Various shades of pink and purple are the most common, but there has been a lot of breeding work on these plants in recent years, and some nurseries offer orange flowers (*Bougainvillea* 'Orange Glow', sold in the United States as *B*. Camarillo Fiesta or *B*. 'Monle'), yellow ('California Gold') and cream ('Easter Parade'). For a real head turner, try *B*. ×*buttiana* 'Raspberry Ice'—it has green and yellow variegated leaves and pink flowers the colour of a late seventies mohican haircut (mohawk).

Another plant that can be brought outdoors for a summer holiday is the wax flower, *Hoya carnosa*. When it is grown in a conservatory you can't really appreciate the flowers, but once it starts scrambling through the branches of a tree, the flowers are clearly visible and carry a delightful scent that is at its strongest at night.

Apart from allowing you to grow two plants in the same space, and adding to the overall spectacle of your garden, growing a climbing houseplant outdoors over summer will do the plants the power of good, resulting in lots of new growth. To get the best out of them, water regularly and feed every two to three weeks with a balanced fertilizer.

A word of warning. Before returning houseplants to their favourite spot indoors, check them for bugs or you will be responsible for introducing all sorts of creatures to your house. There's nothing worse than finding vine weevils crawling up your kitchen wall or spotting slug trails across your dining room table. (Yes, I do speak from experience.)

Small walls or raised structures

Dumpy little walls are not the easiest structures to plant up. Most of the climbing plants that we would grow against tall fences or walls, or train into the branches of trees, have a tendency to romp away like somebody has stuck a rocket under their roots, and will quickly suffocate the wall. The result? Not a pretty sight, and you'll soon become a slave to your hand pruners. Some climbers also look plain wrong. The large leaves of some plants would be completely out of scale with the vertical surface you are trying to cover.

Flanking the edge of the slate path in my garden is an arc of vertical sleepers set in the ground at random heights—at their tallest they come up to my waist, at their lowest, just above my knee. To soften the surfaces of this timber boundary I grow a few climbers, all of which have three attributes: they are self-clinging via adventitious roots (aerial roots), which means I don't need any unsightly wires or a ball of garden twine to keep them in; they are evergreen, giving me patches of colour all year round; and they have dense growth, so they don't bulge out too far and get knocked to smithereens every time somebody walks (or children run excitedly) down the path.

An English ivy with very small leaves has done incredibly well. (I should note, however, that this ivy should not be planted in the Unites States, where it is invasive.) I've absolutely no idea what variety it is—it was bought unnamed in a tiny little pot from the houseplant section of the local garden centre. It was initially shy to form adventitious roots, so I had to give it a helping hand until it had established. As the shoots grew, I tacked them gently to the wall using galvanized U-shaped staples hammered in every 5 cm or so. This helped the ivy make good contact with the wall, and it became established far more quickly this way than it would have if it had been left to its own devices. Don't worry about the staples being conspicuous. With careful placing you won't see them, and they'll soon be hidden by fresh foliage anyway.

Nearby is *Ficus pumila* (creeping fig). Apparently in its native China and Japan this plant can grow up to 10 m, but it is so slow growing that in cooler climates it's unlikely to ever achieve such lofty heights. It's a lovely little thing. The slender stems are clothed in tiny, green, heart-shaped leaves, and it's perfect to grow in shade. I once tried growing *F. pumila* 'Variegata' in the same spot, but it was very disappointing. It

Planting holes have been gouged out at the base of my sleeper wall. Once the holes are planted, slate shingle from the path is used to disguise the soil.

grew at a snail's pace, and sunny spells in early spring seemed to scorch the leaves. Unfortunately, creeping fig is frost tender and only hardy in mild gardens. If you suffer from frost, be prepared to give it some cosseting to help it make it through winter.

Synonymous with the kind of landscaping you would see around car parks and supermarkets, the variegated varieties of *Euonymus fortunei* are the kind of shrubs that most plant lovers sneer at. Gaudy, static and, well, not particularly interesting, they are far too utilitarian for modern gardeners who have an extensive range of sophisticated plants to choose from.

Still, they can make useful climbers. Although members of the *Euonymus fortunei* tribe are most often grown as free-standing shrubs, adventitious roots form on the stems, and in Japan, where it originates, plants are grown at the base of trees to provide a comfy pair of socks to naked trunks. The species is dark green, but if you are looking for something to brighten up a slightly shaded spot, try 'Emerald 'n' Gold' (bright green centre with yellow edges) or Blondy (yellow centre, green margin). A new variety that has been bred in the United States, 'Duncanata Variegated Vegeta', has been described as an exceptionally good climber—it is fairly slow growing with wide white margins and a green heart. Most other forms of *E. fortunei* are also self-climbing, but not all are (including 'Silver Queen'), so do some research before buying.

Trachelospermum jasminoides is a popular scented climber for draping pergolas or smothering a fence, but it is far too aggressive for planting against a small wall. Fortunately you can have all of the scent and less of the vigour by growing *T. asiaticum*. It's much more compact than *T. jasminoides* and has gorgeous, narrow, shiny dark green leaves and emits the rich scent of jasmine from starry, creamy white flowers in summer. Good for sun or partial shade, it's frost hardy, but if you have temperatures of −10°C (14°F) or more, it's not worth trying unless you can give it some protection over the winter months. Sadly it doesn't form adventitious roots, which means you will need to use a training system or pin the stems to the wall. I know it's a bit of a pain, but some plants are worth the extra effort.

Living roofs

It is easy to understand the attraction of a living roof. From my upstairs office window (back bedroom, actually, I'm just trying to sound posh) I have a panoramic view over my neighbours' tiny back gardens, and all of them have one thing in common: a garden shed topped with a sheet of ugly roofing felt. Given the choice of gazing down on this sea of grey or onto a roof planted with flowers, succulents, grasses or bulbs, I'm sure most of us would take the plants without hesitation.

The sedum roof on my small shed is sown with chives to give height to the display and make the most of the space.
Photograph by Alison Reid.

All of these barren shed roofs are candidates for a green roof. While large-scale projects are best undertaken by a skilled specialist, a roof on a small garden building should be simple enough to make in a weekend.

Green roofs have long been popular in other European countries, and now they are popping up everywhere in the United Kingdom, with London alone boasting an estimated 875 square miles of green roof on private and commercial buildings. This includes a 500-square-metre green roof on top of the headquarters of Barclays Bank in Canary Wharf. At 511 feet (156 m), it is Europe's highest living roof and features drought- and wind-tolerant plants.

While a cynic might point out that topping a corporate HQ with plants is an ideal way for a business to boost its green credentials, there is no debate about the environmental advantages of a green roof. The tapestry of plants takes carbon dioxide from the air and absorbs rain water, preventing it running off to drains. Very quickly, a roof will become home to a thriving population of insects, turning it into a magnet for hungry birds.

'Green roof' has become a bit of a catch-all term for any roof that supports

A robotic mower keeps this grass roof at the Yorkshire Sculpture Park in good shape.

plants. The best-known are made with sedum matting, which can be simply rolled out like a piece of carpet onto a prepared roof. Others are planted with wildflowers, drought-tolerant perennials, ornamental grasses, bulbs or annuals. Turf is another option, and I saw a nice example at the Yorkshire Sculpture Park, near Wakefield, which was maintained using a robotic mower.

Providing the structure is not decrepit, you could consider adding a green roof to a shed, hen coop, summer house, home office, child's Wendy house (playhouse) or even a bird table. For sheds and other timber structures, check that the uprights and internal joists are in good order to take the extra weight, and brace the building with more supports if necessary.

The concept of building a roof is more or less the same. The roof will need covering with a sheet of waterproof material (butyl pond liner is ideal), followed by a drainage layer of gravel or custom-made plastic green roof drainage sheeting. Next, a sheet of porous landscape material is added before topping with a layer of moisture-retentive capillary matting. On a flat or low-pitched roof, a timber frame is built around the outside using batons to leave a planting area—the depth will

This amazing green roof by designer Kazuyuki Ishihara was displayed at the 2008 Chelsea Flower Show.

depend on what you want to grow, but sedums need at least 3/4 in. (2 cm) of growing media, while a more diverse mix of flowers and grasses will need nearer 7 in. If your roof has an incline of between twenty and thirty degrees, build the frame and then make an internal grid with batons to create a series of planting pockets. Speak to a specialist if your roof is any steeper than this.

The planting mix you need to fill your frame with will depend on what you want to grow. Experts use all sorts of concoctions with ingredients that include crushed brick, concrete and limestone chippings. Nigel Dunnett, a green roof specialist from the University of Sheffield, covered his shed in a 50:50 mix of expanded clay pellets and loam-based compost, spread in a 4 in. (10 cm) layer.

For simple roofs you can use plug plants, which are very economical, or those grown in small pots. While drought-tolerant plants will look after themselves, some roofs will need watering, which can be accomplished via a computer-controlled leaky pipe irrigation system attached to an outdoor tap. To allow excess water to escape from the drainage layer of the roof, cut or drill holes into the frame.

There is no question that making a large green roof is best left to the professionals, but creating a small roof is something we can all do ourselves. I have made two incredibly simple ones in my garden using Enviromat sedum matting, which contains a mixture of six different succulents. Adding it to my tiny shed was a doddle, taking no longer than an hour. First I laid a sheet of plastic over the roofing felt, then made a frame using 2 in. (5 cm) batons screwed around the edge of the roof. I cut to size a square of capillary matting, or water retention matting, and placed it in the gap. After measuring the recess, I cut a similar-sized piece of matting using a Stanley knife and a steel rule as a straight edge. Another roof on a slightly smaller scale was built using the same process and added to the top of a fence-mounted lacewing chamber.

Although the roof has been doing well, plants do show visible signs of being unhappy in dry weather. This is easily remedied with a bucketful of water, but I wish I'd added a layer of soil-based compost over the capillary matting to give the sedums' roots more space to spread and prevent the plants from drying out so quickly.

A great alternative, if you have the time and patience, is to create your own succulent roof. A few years ago I saw a striking one on top of a shed in a garden at the Chelsea Flower Show. Built by garden designer Teresa Davies, the colourful roof was made from a mixture of twenty tender and hardy succulents, such as aeoniums and large-leaved echeveria.

Davies's construction technique would be ideal for roofs of around one metre square. She starts by covering the roof with a waterproof layer of polythene (polyethylene), then builds a frame with timber batons that are screwed onto the sides,

A living roof is not static. In late spring the sedums in my garden are covered in flowers that attract bees.

front and back. The batons need to be deep enough to ensure that, when in place, there is a 1¹/₂ in. gap between the roof and the top edge of the baton.

The area left within the frame is then measured and a galvanized steel tray is custom built (for the roof I saw, she paid a ventilation equipment company). The tray has drainage holes punched into it, and if it is to go onto a pitched roof, these are at the lowest point.

The tray is placed on a table and ramped up with bricks to match the angle of the roof. Davies adds a lightweight, well-drained mix of compost to the tray (two-thirds multi-purpose compost to one-third vermiculite), leaving a gap of about ¹/₄ in. between the surface of the compost and the lip of the tray.

Working by eye, she starts planting in a corner with *Sedum acre* and then adds houseleeks, combining different varieties to create an attractive pattern. After covering an 8 in. area, she moves on to the other corners before working towards the centre, occasionally dotting in taller, tender succulents, such as purple *Aeonium* 'Zwartkop'. After it is finished, the tray can be lifted into the frame.

Maintaining the roof is easy. It does not need watering unless the plants start to wilt, although tender succulents will need to be removed and placed in a frost-free place over winter.

3
Just Eat It

WHEN I WAS growing up in the 1970s, I can remember squeezing in between my parents on the sofa to watch *The Good Life*, a popular TV sitcom in which a husband and wife give up their comfortable lifestyle with the goal of becoming self-sufficient. Apart from dyeing their own clothes and converting a garden cultivator (rototiller) into an unorthodox mode of transport, they grow all of their own fruit and vegetables by turning their front and back gardens in Surbiton, a commuter town on the outskirts of London, into a market garden. Well, barring the occasional repeat, it's probably been over thirty years since I first sat glued to the show, but the plots of many episodes live in my memory and must surely be partly to blame for my long-harboured ambition to become self-sufficient, like the show's main protagonists, Tom and Barbara Good.

Despite my dreams, I'm realistic enough to know that even if I hoicked out every plant from my tiny garden and replaced them with rows of vegetables, I still wouldn't be able to produce enough to keep my family's hunger pangs at bay for a whole year. However, even if your garden is the size of a postage stamp, it is still possible to grow enough plants to supply food for many meals.

There are many techniques you can use. Some edibles can be grown in pots or tucked into gaps left among ornamental plants. Elsewhere, walls, fences and other vertical surfaces can support fruit-bearing climbing plants or hold the branches of compact, trained forms of fruit tree—all you need to add are some horizontal wires or a trellis.

It only measures 3 ft. by 3 ft., but this square foot potager overflows with colour and tasty goodness. Photograph by Caroline Hughes.

In this tiny courtyard garden there's no soil to grow vegetables in, but the designer has cleverly created raised beds around the outside, leaving plenty of 'living' room in the centre. Photograph by Liz Eddison, courtesy of The Garden Collection.

So what should you grow? Well, that's simple—it's up to you, although I do have a few tips to help with the decision-making process.

- *Only grow what you and your family like to eat.* What's the point of wasting valuable space, time, energy or materials on a crop that is likely to end up on the compost heap? The answer: none at all.

- *Avoid slow-growing crops.* Many vegetables are real plodders, taking about six months from sowing to harvesting. The space they occupy could be used to raise two or three different crops in the same period of time.

- *Go gourmet.* If you're a foodie, it's a great idea to grow some delicacies that you rarely find when shopping or that are likely to burn a hole in your wallet when they do turn up.

- *Hey, good looking.* There's no room for utilitarian crops in a small space. Even edible crops have to possess some attractive qualities, whether it's the shape or colour of the foliage, gorgeous flowers, striking stems or the yummy end product.

- *Include a few perennials.* Most owners of tiny gardens would rather devote space to ornamentals than to perennial fruit, vegetables and herbs, but I grow a few for several reasons: as the plants mature the harvest is more bountiful, I use the end product frequently in my kitchen and once planted, these plants provide food with minimum effort expended on my part (allowing me to channel my energy elsewhere).

- *Don't overdo it.* Flick through the pages of a seed or fruit catalogue and you'll be faced with a mouth-watering selection of plants to grow. Speaking from experience, it's all too easy to get carried away and order more than you can grow or have room for. Be selective, work out where you are going to plant perennials and after making an initial list, revisit your wish list and edit it down.

- *Plan for the year.* The majority of edible plants will be ready for picking in the summer and autumn, but you can extend the season by making later sowings, using cloches for protection to provide food in winter or by growing perennial herbs that will provide pickings all year round.

As far as I'm concerned, eating your own fruit and vegetables is one of life's greatest pleasures, and you really can enjoy an exciting mix of crops in a Lilliputian space. In fact, you can raise your own food even if the only garden you have is a balcony or window box. Don't believe me? Well, for many years I lived on the third storey of a block of flats and managed to grow enough basil plants on two sunny windowsills to enable me to make several jars of pesto sauce. Delicious!

Making the most of your space

When I first moved into my house in East London, the tiny terraced garden I inherited was loosely enclosed by a few saggy wires threaded between some upright concrete posts. Due to its porosity, we got to know our neighbours well (nobody had fences), but it provided easy access for local foxes and restricted the opportunity to grow climbing plants or those that need some form of support. Much to the displeasure of my neighbours, who thought I was trying to shut them out, I spent a few weeks erecting a close-board fence around my plot.

Now I had gained three more vertical surfaces, and my plan was to use the fence to support a mixture of edible plants that could be grown fairly close to it, ensuring that they would not take up value bed growing space.

Taking pride of place is a Black Hamburgh dessert grape vine that thrives on the east-facing side of the garden. This is one of my favourite plants, and it comes from great stock. In 2003, when I worked as features editor for the *BBC Gardeners' World* magazine, the best-selling gardening title in the United Kingdom, I visited Hampton Court Palace to interview the keeper of the Great Vine, then a 235-year-old *Vitis vinifera* Black Hamburgh (now known by the rather less romantic name 'Schiava Grossa') that was reputedly planted by Lancelot 'Capability' Brown in 1768. The vine is truly breath-taking, with a trunk 5 ft. (1.5 m) in circumference and a spread of about 120 ft. (36.5 m). I was the first journalist to discover that this world-famous vine was going to be propagated, allowing gardeners to grow the progeny of this unique plant for themselves. I expressed my excitement at the news, and a few months later a package arrived in the post containing my very own rooted cutting.

Despite growing best in a warm greenhouse, the vine has thrived outdoors with no protection (other than a thick mulch of manure spread across the root zone in autumn) and is usually festooned with twenty or so bunches of plump black grapes covered in an attractive, sugary bloom. These are really tasty, although my children prefer the insipid green beads of water sold in supermarkets, solely because they don't have any seeds in them.

I grow my vine in the area between two fence posts, which roughly measures 6 ft. by 6 ft. (1.8 m by 1.8 m), using the double Guyot method (sometimes called cane pruning), which is perfect in a small garden as it allows me to keep it confined between the fence posts.

To train a grape vine using this method, start by fitting four horizontal training wires to your fence. Use heavy-duty 12-gauge wire secured by eye bolts. The first wire should be 16 in. (41 cm) from the ground and the rest spaced 12 in. (30 cm) apart. These should be tight enough not to bow under the weight of the stems, but not overly taut as this will put too much strain on the fence. If you have heavy clay soil, like I do, improve it before planting by digging in plenty of well-rotted manure along with several handfuls of horticultural grit.

In late autumn dig a hole 6 in. (15 cm) away from the fence and plant the vine at the same level as it was growing before. Insert a 6 ft. (1.8 m) garden cane behind the vine and secure it to the training wires. Cut the vine back hard to 6 in. (15 cm) above the ground.

Next season, allow only one stem to grow, pruning all side shoots to one leaf. In November, cut back hard to three healthy buds beneath the bottom wire. Allow three stems to grow (from the healthy buds) and secure them to the cane. Prune any side shoots to one leaf and remove flowers.

A year later, in November, select two shoots and tie them down to the bottom

My Black Hamburgh grapes (*Vitis vinifera* 'Schiava Grossa') are ready for picking in early autumn.

wire on either side of the central stem. Reduce their length to around 29 in. (74 cm) and prune the remaining stem, leaving three or four buds to form shoots the next season.

From spring, shoots will grow from the horizontal branches. You need 6 in. (15 cm) gaps between shoots, so prune out any that are too congested or that are growing towards the fence. Regularly tie shoots to the wires and prune side shoots to one leaf. When the slender stems reach the top wire, remove the growing tips.

Many other vines are suitable for this growing method, including *Vitis* 'Glenora', an American variety with black fruit, green seedless *V.* 'Himrod' and *V.* 'Schuyler', which has black grapes and striking red autumn foliage.

As a child I thought apricots came sliced in tins. For many years these slivers of gold, drowning in thick syrupy juice, were a delicious treat that my mother would pile high above meringue nests before smothering them with cream. This was once the only way to buy them, but then dried apricots appeared and now they are widely available fresh. Like most 'exotic' fruit, the majority of apricots are shipped into the United Kingdom, which accounts for their high price. This leads most people to believe that they can't be grown successfully in our climate.

Well, thanks to modern breeding work there are now several varieties that will

If you can protect apricot blossoms from frost and the developing fruit from squirrels, you will have enough fruit for a good pie.

do well in a cool climate, as long as the apricots are given a sunny, sheltered spot in the garden. I grow Flavorcot in a 5$^{1}/_{2}$-gallon (25-litre) pot, which has been secured against a west-facing fence (to stop it blowing over in a strong gust), almost directly opposite my vine. Bought as a bare-root plant, it has been fan trained with canes inserted in the pot and bound together with twine.

It's an easy plant to grow. I protect the buds and flowers from frost with a giant 'sock' made from horticultural fleece (cover cloth), which can be lifted on and off the plant easily and tied at the bottom to prevent it blowing off in the wind. When the baby fruit are about the size of a fingernail, thinning is required to leave fruit about 4 in. (10 cm) apart. It's then a case of chasing off pesky grey squirrels, who will quickly strip a tree of fruit, and waiting for the apricots to ripen. Flavorcot is generally ready to be picked in June, and in most years it has provided me with around thirty fruit. Another apricot suitable for fan training is 'Tomcot', but you could also try similar glamorous fruit, such as peaches, nectarines and figs, or something more traditional like a cherry.

Not all my fruit plants grown against the fence have been a resounding success. When I planted up a small, rectangular bed that sits adjacent to my patio with small specimens of *Astelia chathamica* 'Silver Spear', *Correa* 'Marian's Marvel' and *Euphorbia mellifera*, I underestimated how quickly they would grow and planted a self-fertile Chinese gooseberry, or kiwifruit (*Actinidia deliciosa* 'Jenny'), in the space behind. It speedily twinned itself along the network of wires I'd installed, but within a couple of seasons it was lost behind the shrubs. Deprived of light, it will never boast the huge clusters of egg-shaped, hairy fruit that I've seen in books, but I still love its fabulous large leaves that smother the long stems clothed with beautiful red hairs. If planted in a sunny, light spot, it would be perfect for a small garden as it can be tightly confined against a wall or fence.

After using up all the decent fence growing space, I still wanted to grow other fruit that would need a vertical support, such as raspberries. These are generally not ideal for a small garden as they have a tendency to spread and are only attractive when they're in fruit, but they're a firm favourite with my family so I decided to find a way to squeeze one in. My solution was to grow a single plant against a tree stake planted in my greenhouse bed. They love well-drained soil, so I dug in some horticultural grit before hammering a square-sided 6 ft. stake into the bed. (Make sure the stake is in a position that's accessible, as this will make it easier to tie in canes regularly, pick fruit and snip off any wayward canes to restrict its growth.)

There are many raspberries worth growing. Some bear fruit in summer, others in autumn, while some produce a crop in both seasons. I grow *Rubus idaeus* 'Glen Ample', a thornless variety that boasts bright red berries in summer. If you want something really showy, try the gleaming yellow *R. idaeus* 'All Gold'.

Filling the gaps

Bare patches of earth between ornamental plants in beds or borders are perfect to plug with perennial or annual edible plants, which have to look good and, most importantly, taste good. I grow feathery bronze fennel (*Foeniculum vulgare* 'Purpureum') in a space at the back of my raised bed, between my fence and *Cercis canadensis* 'Forest Pansy'—the large, heart-shaped, purple leaves of the small tree contrast well with the delicate foliage of the fennel. The foliage of this tall but airy perennial is lovely chopped into salads, and the clump looks great from spring to autumn, when it is topped by large, flattened heads of yellow flowers. Later you can either collect the seed for use in the kitchen or allow the plant to self-seed—but be warned, you'll have to remove the seeds rigorously, as they will pop up everywhere.

Many perennial herbs could be considered for the small garden. If you have a gap at the edge of a path, check out *Rosmarinus officinalis* Prostratus Group 'Capri', a ground-covering rosemary whose trailing stems are clothed in dark green, edible needles and masses of blue flowers in summer—its evergreen foliage ensures that it still adds verdant colour in the depths of winter. Alternatively, there are many thymes that would grow equally well in such a position. Taller-growing plants to chew over include *Achillea ageratum* (mace), which has handsome, slender-toothed leaves and sprays of white flowers, *Salvia officinalis* 'Icterina' (golden variegated sage) and *Phlomis italica*, a compact, narrow-leaved form of Jerusalem sage.

The sheer number of vegetables and herbs that are available to grow from seed means that there is a huge opportunity to experiment with annuals as gap fillers. Among my favourites are Florence fennel (*Foeniculum vulgare* var. *azoricum*), which is technically biennial but is grown as an annual for its distinctive swollen white bulb, which sits beneath a mound of delicate fern-like foliage. Many types of chard will turn heads, but the most colourful stems can be found in Swiss chard 'Bright Lights'—this seed mixture packs in seven zingy colours, including red, yellow, orange and purple.

Kale 'Black Tuscany', or black kale, is a tasty vegetable that fortunately also has the more palatable common name of cavelo nero (or cavolo nero). It's a dramatic plant that makes an upright rosette of dark green, almost black, strap-like leaves that are deeply puckered. As it overwinters well, it's perfect to cheer up the garden and plate at this bleak time of year.

Leafy salads are one of the best edibles to squeeze into tight gaps, especially those that can be picked as cut-and-come-again crops to prevent them growing to their mature size. Grow single plants of good-looking lettuces, such as crinkly, deep red 'Lollo Rosso' (or 'Lollo Rossa') or 'Freckles', which has dark green leaves that look as if they have been splattered with red paint. Alternatively, make the most of a gap of any size by sowing rows of mixed salad leaves, mustard, coriander (cilantro), rocket (also known as arugula, rucola and roquette) or variegated land cress, which has green and yellow leaves and a taste similar to watercress. Apart from making good use of empty space, a crop of salad leaves will have the added advantage of preventing weeds from germinating on bare soil.

Before planting in the soil, prepare the ground by forking it over and raking to leave a fine finish. Next, make shallow trenches about ¹/₂ in. (1.25 cm) deep and spread seed thinly along the bottom. Cover with soil and water. When seedlings are about 1 in. (2.5 cm) tall, thin them out to give them space to grow (the distance will depend on the variety).

Edibles for shade

A problem with many small gardens is that they can be very shady, especially if you garden in a city. Trees in the neighbour's garden, a heavy concentration of buildings or a north-facing aspect can make some small spaces very gloomy—not the ideal conditions for growing most fruit and vegetables.

Any gaps beneath other plants in borders can be plugged with shade-tolerant vegetables and herbs. Photograph by Alison Reid.

If this is the case, should you just give up on the idea of growing your own crops in the shade? Of course not! But you do need to be realistic and understand that you will never be able to pick from the huge range of plants available to those with a sunny space.

Perhaps the most rewarding crops to grow in shady gardens are salads. Lettuces and mixed leaf blends are ideal as they grow quickly and will not run to seed as fast in shade as they do in full sun.

Several herbs will also do well. Chives, coriander and parsley are ideal. Mint will also romp away in shade, but as it can become extremely invasive, either grow it in an aboveground pot or in a pot plunged into the soil, with the edge just above the surface to prevent it from escaping into the soil.

If you want to grow fruit, try alpine strawberries. Naturally a woodland plant, it prefers moist, cool, shady conditions. I've planted several in a large strawberry planter that sits under a shrub.

Red and white currants are useful plants for shaded sites and could be grown against walls and fences. Blackberries will do okay in slight shade, as will blueberries, although both plants produce a better crop in sun.

Even if you're lucky enough not to have a completely shaded garden, you will

A pot planted with alpine strawberries will do well in shade.

probably have a few dark spots under a shrub or at the base of wall. If you really want to make the most of your space, you could try filling them with some of these edible crops.

Vegetables in pots

When I started out as a professional gardener back in 1988, nobody grew vegetables in pots (at least I can't remember anyone doing it). The only folk who could enjoy picking fruit and vegetables they had raised themselves were the old boys on the allotment and those with a large enough garden to have a dedicated vegetable patch, or if they were extremely posh, their own kitchen garden (walled, of course). In fact, growing vegetables was seen as quite an antiquated pastime back then, lacking the sophistication and glamour of raising flowers. I even remember one gardening magazine editor telling me that he would never put vegetables on the front cover of his title as it would stymie sales because "our readers don't grow vegetables".

How things change. Photographs of artistically composed edible crops are often splashed across the covers of mainstream gardening magazines, while there are plenty of specialist titles entirely dedicated to growing your own produce. And if further evidence was needed to prove how vegetables have entered the main-

In late winter I start many of my vegetable plants off from seed sown in the greenhouse.

stream, then a quick word with our leading seed companies reveals that sales of vegetable seeds are almost outstripping flower seeds, something that has never happened before. Many of the increasing range sold by seed companies are aimed specifically at those of us with tiny gardens, whether it's a courtyard, patio, roof garden or even a balcony.

Choosing pots

Choose containers that are large enough for the eventual size of your plant. Many compact herbs are ideal in small pots, but most vegetables need a large pot, 8–17 in. (20–45 cm) in diameter. This will give the roots plenty of space to spread and help to provide a stable support to top-heavy plants that become laden with produce and are vulnerable to being blown over. Plastic pots are cheap, but glazed or plain terracotta win when it comes to looks. However, the porous nature of these pots means the compost will dry out quickly, so to prevent a check to the growth of plants and to cut down on the amount of watering you have to carry out, line the inside of the pot with polythene (polyethylene), pierced at the base to assist drainage.

Growing bags have long been used by gardeners starved of space, but I've found an ingenious bag that will take up even less room in the garden. The Kayak Growbag made by Vital Earth starts life on the garden centre shelf looking like any

The slimline Kayak Growbag fits neatly against a wall.

other growing bag, but is easily transformed when you get it home. You start by giving it a good shake to break up the peat-free compost, then turn it on its side and it shrinks in width by half. At the same time the depth of compost is doubled, giving you a deeper root run and hopefully better vegetables. Oh, and it also looks a bit like a boat, hence the name.

What to grow

There's a massive choice of crops that can be grown in pots. It's best to try compact plants such as sweet peppers, chilli peppers (chiles) and aubergines (eggplant) rather than tall-growing vegetables like Brussels sprouts, which demand lots of water and can be blown down easily. Among the best for pots are courgettes, beetroot, carrots, squash, kale 'Black Tuscany', Florence fennel (*Foeniculum vulgare* var. *azoricum*) and potatoes. Herbs can be planted on their own or you could try growing ten different sorts in the planting pockets of a strawberry planter—this is an ideal trick to squeeze a high density of plants into the meanest of gardens, or where it would be impossible to find room for lots of pots, such as on a narrow balcony. Most plants are ideal in multi-purpose compost, but some have special needs. For instance, thyme prefers fairly well drained soil and is best in a soil-based compost.

Leafy salads are among the most satisfying plants to grow, as all will be ready to harvest within three weeks of being sown—and because they are really tasty and

Left: The clever handles on this potato-growing sack enable you to transport the sack easily to another part of the garden.

Right: Egg-sized potato 'Mimi' is harvested.

extremely good for you, this must make them the ultimate in fast food. Among those worth trying are Niche Salad Leaves Blend, which is a lively mixture of radish leaf, carrot leaves, red amaranth, golden purslane, wrinkled cress, salad burnet and kale 'Red Russian'. Oriental saladini has an Eastern flavour, featuring pak choi (bok choy), komatsuna, Chinese cabbage, mizuna, and green and purple mustard. Elsewhere, the Italian Salad Collection is a tasty mixture of basil, chicory, lettuce

If you only have room for one pot, try growing nine different herbs in a strawberry planter.

'Lollo Rosso' ('Lollo Rossa'), radicchio and rocket. (Herby Salad Leaf Mixed is a similar alternative.)

Other salads that deserve to be grown are rocket, salad bowl lettuce and corn salad, which has small, sweet leaves. The leaves of finely divided mizuna look great on the plate, while beet 'Bull's Blood' has burgundy red leaves and a mild beetroot flavour. If you prefer your salads to have a bit of a kick, there are plenty of mustard leaves on the market, including 'Red Frills', which has feathery leaves, 'Pizzo', whose bright green leaves are attractively serrated and 'Giant Red', whose spicy leaves are ideal for stir-fries. (If 'Red Frills' is unavailable in your area, try the comparable 'Ruby Streaks', and 'Golden Frill' is a suitable alternative for 'Pizzo'.)

It's also possible to make extra use of space by combining several different plants in the same pot. For instance, dwarf French bean works well with lettuce and nasturtium, which has edible flowers with a slight peppery taste. I saw another great combination on a visit to Petersham Nurseries, near Richmond, south-west London, where they grow a lot of edible plants in pots for use in their acclaimed restaurant: the head gardener had planted a purple basil in the centre of a pot surrounded by lower-growing marjoram. There are lots of plants that would work well together, and it's great to experiment. As with any kind of mixed planting, it will work best if there is a plant to provide height, a plant to occupy the middle ground and a prostrate vegetable or edible flower to trail around the edge.

Plants or seeds?

For the greatest choice of vegetables, it is best to browse through mail-order catalogues and grow your own from seed. However, if you forget to order seed, don't have enough time to grow them yourself or are not too bothered about the variety, buy ready-grown plants from garden centres or specialist growers. Most vegetable seeds will need sowing in early spring so that you'll have decent-sized plants ready to go into pots in late spring or early summer.

How to plant

Mix a handful of water-retaining crystals into your compost and fill your chosen pot to the top. Gently tap to settle the compost and firm down with your fingertips to leave a level surface. Aim to leave a 1 in. gap between the surface of the compost and the lip of the pot. Scoop out compost in the centre of the pot to leave a hole slightly bigger than the root ball of your plant. Remove its pot and place it in the hole. Replace compost around the plant and firm, making sure the surface of the plant is level with the top of the compost. If you are growing leafy salads, either scatter seeds thinly across the surface of the pot or sow in rows, covering the seeds with compost and watering.

Aftercare

To enable plants to thrive, water their containers regularly and don't allow the compost to dry out. Some fruit-forming vegetables, such as tomatoes and peppers, will also enjoy being fed every week with a fertilizer high in potash. Liquid tomato food is perfect and can be applied effectively with a watering can.

Many vegetables have specific needs when it comes to care, but generally, leafy herbs and vegetables need picking regularly to ensure they remain compact and productive, and removing flower buds from these plants will allow them to focus their energy on making masses of new foliage rather than on producing unwanted seeds. Once plants start to do this, they lose vigour and the taste will be tainted. Taller-growing plants like tomatoes, aubergines and peppers will also need staking with canes to prevent the stems from snapping under the weight of their fruit.

If you've used fresh compost, it's unlikely that you'll have much of a problem with weeds, but it's important to tug out any that appear. Not only do you run the risk of them flowering and setting seed elsewhere, but they can also cause a check to the growth of your vegetables by greedily sucking up the moisture from the pot.

Growing vegetables in pots doesn't mean they will escape the gamut of pests and diseases, and they are just as vulnerable as veggies growing in the soil, but many problems can be nipped in the bud if they are spotted early enough. Slugs and snails are the greatest menace in my garden. Although I'm resigned to great chunks being bitten out of my plants, I do find I can minimize the damage by patrolling my crops regularly and dispatching any that I find with a satisfying crunch of my heel.

Fruit in pots

If you want to be self-sufficient in apples, pears, nectarines and figs, it helps to have a well-stocked orchard, but you don't need rolling acres or a country estate to grow fruit. It's possible to grow a wide range of varieties in the smallest of spaces by raising plants in pots.

In my own garden, which measures just 30 ft. by 15 ft., I have managed to squeeze in eleven different fruit, which thrive in large containers—there's a fig, blackberry, red currant, pomegranate, apricot, loquat, blueberry, olive, strawberries, alpine strawberries and lots of cranberries. Okay, I admit that a couple of these don't reliably produce fruit in our climate, and a single plant is never going to provide me

My cordon red currant produces jewel-like berries.

Strawberries flank the side of my raised sleeper bed.

Pomegranates won't produce fruit unless you live in a warm climate or grow them in a heated greenhouse, but they are still worth growing for their attractive red flowers.

It may not produce edible fruit, but hardy banana (*Musa basjoo*) is an imposing architectural plant.

with a glut, but picking anything you have grown yourself is incredibly rewarding and always tastes better than something you have had to pay for.

When to plant

While many fruit plants can be bought in containers throughout the year, the best time to buy trees is during the autumn, when nurseries offer a wide range of bare-root plants. These are cheaper to buy than container-grown plants and will quickly romp away when put in a pot. Although planting of bare-root trees can carry on until early spring (as long as the soil isn't frozen or waterlogged), many of the best plants are quickly snapped up, so it pays to order your plants as early as possible.

Choosing pots and planting

As with vegetables, you can use either plastic or terracotta pots. Both have advantages and disadvantages, but the most important thing is to ensure that whatever you use has adequate drainage at the base, as waterlogged roots will soon kill the plant. Choose pots that are 12–17 in. (30–45 cm) in diameter, or bigger if the plant demands it, and fill with a loam-based compost. Mix a handful of controlled-release fertilizer granules into the compost before planting, which will help to feed the plants for several months. After planting, keep the compost moist but not soaking, allowing the surface to dry out before watering again.

What to grow

So what should you grow? Well, this largely depends on personal preference. There are plenty of traditional and more exotic fruit you could try. However, some plants will sulk when confined to a pot, including most plums, cherries, grapes, currants, blackberries and raspberries.

Many varieties of apple can be grown well in a small space, such as on patios and balconies. Probably the best way of growing this popular fruit is to find room for a duo-minarette, a special tree that forms a vertical stem and only reaches 4 ft. (1.2 m) after ten years. Rather than make spreading branches, it forms stumpy little shoots that hold the fruit only a few centimetres from the stem. Each tree has been propagated to bear two varieties of apple, for instance 'Cox's Orange Pippin' and 'Falstaff', or 'James Grieve' and 'Winter Gem', a large pink-flushed apple with an aromatic flavour.

Pears are also available as duo-minarettes, and a popular double act that grow on the same tree are 'Conference' and 'Concorde'. Alternatively, dwarf pear 'Terrace

Pearl' is extremely compact and grows to 4 ft. (1.2 m). It's really easy to look after as it needs very little pruning, and it is very attractive—the branches are smothered in white flowers during the spring, and the fruit, which are ready to pick in the autumn, are long, green and narrow.

If planted directly into the ground, figs will grow rampantly and if left unpruned will produced tiny, hard fruit only fit for the compost bin. However, they are ideal for large containers, which keep the roots restricted and enable the branches to be dealt with easily. *Ficus carica* 'Brown Turkey' is the most commonly grown variety, but my favourite is *F. carica* 'Brunswick' due its most fantastic, deeply lobed leaves and delicious fruit.

In the tiniest garden every plant has to earn its keep, and wherever you can, it makes sense to use every inch of your space. A great way of doing this it to grow several plants in the same pot. For instance, gooseberries, such as 'Invicta', which has heavy crops of pale green berries from mid-summer, and 'Remarka', whose dark red fruit have smooth skins, can be bought as half standards (a plant with a clear stem and a lollipop-shaped head) and underplanted with herbs.

Another good idea is to put plants together that like the same soil. I grow *Vaccinium* 'Chandler' (blueberry) in the centre of a pot filled with ericaceous compost (with added grit to improve the drainage) and have planted *V. macrocarpon* 'Red Star'

Pinch the tips of figs back for a bushy plant, and feed often for a bumper crop of fruit.

(cranberry) around the edges. This combination gives a long season of interest—the blueberry boasts flowers in the spring, followed by summer fruit, while the cranberry has evergreen foliage that cascades down the sides of the pot and is clad in glossy red berries during the autumn. My original aim was to grow enough to make my own cranberry sauce at Christmas, but unless you can dedicate several large pots to their production, you will still have to supplement your supply with a few bags from the supermarket. If you have a greenhouse, it's a good idea to move the blueberry pot inside over winter, but I leave mine outside and protect it from frost by covering it with a sheet of horticultural fleece (cover cloth).

Many berry-bearing plants will do well. Blackberries can quickly become unruly thugs and generally need to be tamed by training against a system of horizontal wires. However, for the last couple of years I've been growing 'Loch Maree', an excellent variety that is perfectly behaved. It thrives in sun or slight shade and produces super-sweet, juicy berries, but it also has a couple of other attributes that make it worth growing: the stems are easy to handle, as they are completely thornless, and the flowers that appear in spring are double pink.

Although you could grow this blackberry against supports attached to a wall or fence, I've planted mine in a $3^1/_2$-gallon (15-litre) pot filled with a loam-based compost. As the stems grow I tie them in to a 6 ft. (1.8 m) garden cane pushed into the container. This method makes it possible for anyone with a patio or even a balcony to grow this fruit.

Lots of tender fruit that we associate with warmer climates will do well in pots if given a sunny, sheltered spot. Peaches, apricots and nectarines are all ideal and can be fan trained, which makes a neat, compact tree that can be pushed up against a fence or wall. To do this, push two canes into the compost behind the plant to make a V shape and then tie the canes horizontally to the V. Tasty varieties to try are nectarine 'Lord Napier', which has pale green flesh, and peach 'Peregrine', whose white flesh is incredibly juicy. My favourite apricot is Flavorcot, which I grow in a $3^1/_2$-gallon (15-litre) pot, and there are also dwarf varieties that can be allowed to grow as open bushes, reaching only 5 ft. (1.5 m) after ten years. This includes nectarine 'Nectarella', peach 'Bonanza' and apricot 'Garden Aprigold', which has large orange fruit. While these fruit are easy to grow, they do need a certain amount of protection from frost, especially when they have come into flower in early spring. Put them in a greenhouse or on a porch, or cover with horticultural fleece.

While some trees have a prolific bounty, others are worth growing for their foliage or flowers. The twisted stems and grey leaves of olives evoke the spirit of Tuscany and look wonderful in pots, but don't expect to make your own first cold pressing of extra virgin olive oil, as they rarely produce worthwhile fruit in the United Kingdom or other temperate areas. Having said that, I have high hopes for

Opposite: Olive 'Veronique' is ideal for the variable UK climate. It produced a mass of fruit in its first summer in my garden.

Olea europaea 'Veronique', a new variety hardy to −20°C (−4°F) that reportedly produces a reasonable crop of fruit in our summers.

Another pretty tree is the pomegranate. I grow one in a terracotta pot and love its glossy leaves and waxy red flowers that appear in early summer. However, pomegranates rarely produce full-size fruit outside in the United Kingdom, and mine fall off when they reach the size of a ping-pong ball.

Most gardens, however small, have enough space for at least one type of fruit, whether it's a tree, bush or just a few strawberries growing in a tower-style planter. If you've never grown your own before, give it a go, but be realistic. You're never going to have enough varieties for a decent fruit salad, but picking your own juicy fruit straight from the plant is one of gardening's joys.

Micro leaves

If you are flush enough to be able to dine in a fashionable restaurant, you may have been served a dish embellished with micro leaves—vegetable seedlings that are harvested six to twenty-one days after germination. Also known as micro greens, living greens or micro herbs (they're so new that nobody has decided on a catch-all

Micro leaves in the greenhouse give us something tasty to eat over winter.

name yet), these are loved by leading chefs in the United Kingdom and United States for their flavour, which is more intense than that of the fully grown plant.

Unlike sprouting seeds, which are soaked in water and then left to sprout in special trays, micro leaves are grown in compost, vermiculite or on special absorbent mats. They're a doddle to grow and perfect for the most space-strapped gardener. In autumn and winter I grow mine on the kitchen windowsill or on the staging in my greenhouse, but in summer they can be put outdoors to bask in the sun.

The seedlings can be sprinkled onto soup, added to sandwiches or scattered over a salad to help give it a lift, and there are plenty to try. Among my favourites are sunflower, snow pea (also called Chinese pea and usually grown for its edible pods), Oregon sugar pod pea, fennel, coriander, celery, Genovese basil, chervil, broccoli and rocket. Some have really colourful stems and leaves, which look great on the plate. Among the most striking are purple radish, red mustard, beetroot and Swiss chard 'Bright Lights'.

The great thing about micro leaves is that they can be grown all year round, even during the depths of winter when there's little else to pick outside. The only downside to growing them during the cooler months, when daylight hours are shorter and light intensity is lower, is that they will take slightly longer to develop than those sown during the spring and summer.

Growing them is foolproof. You can use a standard or half-size seed tray, or do your bit for the environment by using old margarine tubs, yoghurt cartons or the plastic punnets (baskets) used for packaging fruit in the supermarket—no special treatment is needed, just give them a quick swill under the tap to remove any residues. The depth of the container isn't that important, but having adequate drainage is. If the tray doesn't have any holes, add a few underneath with a skewer.

Next, fill the bottom of the container with about an inch of growing media. Professional growers, who supply restaurants or delicatessens with seedlings, use special mats or compost, but I prefer to use vermiculite as it's sterile, easy to handle and doesn't harbour waterborne fungal diseases, such as damping off, which could wipe out your crop. Firm the vermiculite down with your fingertips to leave a roughly flat surface, then sow the seeds, scattering liberally over the surface of the compost (there's no need to cover). For a really good harvest, ensure that the seeds are almost touching. Yes, I know this is bad horticultural practice, but the seeds will only grow for a few days, so don't worry about it. Although most seeds can be sown dry, plump seeds, such as peas, will germinate more readily if soaked overnight in a cup of water.

After sowing, pour some water onto a saucer and set the container on top, allowing the water to be soaked up by the sponge-like vermiculite. Add more water until the surface is visibly wet. To germinate, place the container in a light, warm place. In winter a windowsill is ideal, as long it is not directly above a radiator or next to a draughty windowpane. To ensure a good crop, keep a close eye on water and add more to the saucer if the top dries out.

Your micro leaves will be ready to pick when they reach the first cotyledon stage—generally six to twenty-one days after sowing, with the majority of summer-sown crops reaching their peak after ten days. In winter the same plants can take four or more days longer. In my experience, some seeds are not worth growing over winter. Basil, which tends to be a bit of a dawdler, can take up to three weeks to reach harvestable seedling size during summer, but will take considerably longer in winter. Why attempt to raise a slow-growing crop when there are so many other crops that will germinate readily?

Micro leaves really are tasty, and as you become more successful in growing them you may become tempted to experiment with other vegetables. Although many other veggies are bound to produce a tasty crop, I would suggest only growing what has been recommended or what you see for sale as sprouting seeds or micro leaves in shops—some seedlings are known to taste disgusting, and others, such as parsnips, can cause an upset stomach. Still, there are scores that can be grown safely. For a good supply of leaves, try sowing a tray or two every week.

Square foot gardening

I'd love to be able to take credit for inventing 'square foot gardening' but I can't. This space-saving method of growing vegetables originates from the United States, and I first found out about it after browsing the Web in the early 2000s. Since then I've become a devotee of this innovative way of growing, which allows you to raise lots of crops in the smallest garden by using a raised bed split into a series of 1 ft. by 1 ft. (30 cm by 30 cm) squares with a different plant grown in each.

My bed is only 3 ft. by 3 ft. (90 cm by 90 cm), which may seem small, yet it allows me to grow nine different vegetables. If you have a larger garden you could increase the dimensions of the bed slightly, say to 4 ft. by 4 ft. (1.2 m by 1.2 m), or 5 ft. by 4 ft. (1.5 m by 1.2 m). However, it's important not to make the bed too large, as you need to be able to reach into the centre of it to remove weeds, add water, carry out maintenance work and, of course, pick your crops.

After building a bed, you could site it on a sunny patio (mine is within easy reach of the kitchen) or near to an outdoor cooking area, allowing the chef to pluck vegetables or herbs straight from the bed to add to meals cooked on the barbecue. I've also seen pictures of beds on lawns, but I think this only worth doing if you plan to leave the bed in position permanently, as you will quickly end up with a square patch of dead grass.

Making the bed

If you have a pile of old bricks at hand, a simple bed can be made by laying two or three courses of bricks, staggering the joints in a stretcher bond pattern. Unless you want a permanent structure, lay the bricks dry, without the use of mortar, which will make it easy to dismantle them at the end of the growing season or transport them to another part of the garden. Another option is to buy a raised bed kit. There are several on the market that are really simple to build by connecting ready-cut boards together with dowels.

Alternatively, if you can spare an hour or so, it's simple to make a tough, long-lasting raised bed by putting together lengths of new or recycled timber. Building your own requires only the most basic DIY skills. Here's my recipe to construct a 3 ft. by 3 ft. (90 cm by 90 cm) bed.

The ingredients

Lengths of 9 in. by 2 in. (23 cm by 5 cm) timber for the sides of the bed
Lengths of 2 in. by 2 in. (5 cm by 5 cm) timber for the corner stakes
Sixteen 3 in. (8 cm) wood screws
Saw
Drill
$^{13}/_{64}$ in. (4 mm) drill bit
Countersink drill bit
Pencil
Tri-square
Screwdriver

Cut the planks to length for the frame. You will have two 3 ft. (90 cm) pieces and two 2 ft. 8 in. (80 cm) pieces. Next, cut four corner stakes 9 in. (23 cm) long. Make pencil marks 2 in. (5 cm) from the edge on the 3 ft. sides. Place a stake against the side and line it up with the mark. Drill through the side, countersink to ensure the head of the screw sits flush, then screw the side and stake together. Continue in this way until you have built a square frame. After building your bed, you may wish to apply preservative if the timber is untreated. I finished mine by painting it a recessive mossy green similar to the colour of my fence.

Preparing the bed

What growing media should you use? Well, don't be tempted to quarry your own garden soil for the raised bed, as the growth of seeds will be patchy and you'll be providing free transport for any bug, beastie, weed or disease that resides below the ground. I make my own mix using 50 percent sterilized topsoil and 50 percent multi-purpose compost, along with a few added handfuls of sharp horticultural grit to improve drainage (I do this by eye and don't use any complicated mathematical formula to work it out). To ensure the grit assists rather than hinders drainage, wash it a few times to remove any residues—it's a piece of cake to do this by punching a few holes in the base of the bag and running a hosepipe through the top so the debris runs out the bottom. As most of the crops you will be growing in the raised bed will be fairly shallow rooting, you don't need to fill the frame with any more than about 6 in. of your compost mix.

As my garden seems to be a maternity ward for slugs and snails, I finish my bed by attaching a band of sticky-backed copper tape (bought from a supplier of organic gardening products) around the outside of it. Any pesky mollusc that tries to crawl up the bed is repelled by a tiny, natural electric charge emitted by the copper. This may sound far-fetched, but it really does work, and the only time the slippery menaces manage to invade my bed is when the branches from nearby shrubs arch over due to heavy rain and form a bridge for them to cross. As much as I'm loath to prune unnecessarily, I will sometimes snip away at nearby branches just to prevent this from happening.

What to grow

The trick with square foot gardening is to select varieties that are shallow rooting, compact and that do not spread too much. Despite these limitations, it can still be difficult to decide what to grow, as there are hundreds of tempting plants to choose from. My advice is to pick gourmet varieties rather than run-of-the-mill crops, and plants that will give you tasty pickings for a number of months rather than a glut over a couple of weeks.

You could just grow a random selection of crops, but I think it's much better fun to give the bed a theme, depending on the kind of food you like to eat. For instance, if you're a Francophile you could try carrot 'Parisier Market', endive 'En Cornet de Bordeaux', long shallot 'Jermor' (or the comparable shallot 'Banana'), Swiss chard of Lyon, French sorrel, garlic 'Lautrec Wight', tomato 'Marmande', radish 'Plum Purple' and chervil. Alternatively, if you like oriental nosh, make a bed with Thai basil, lemon grass, Chinese radish, chilli pepper 'Thai Dragon', coriander, ori-

A band of copper stuck around the outside of my square foot garden protects the crops from leaf-munching slugs and snails.

ental mustards, Japanese bunching onion and oriental spinach. As a lover of Italian food I recently devoted my bed to varieties that herald from this gastronomic country. Rubbing shoulders with Genovese basil, chilli pepper 'Pinocchio's Nose', plum tomato 'Roma' and aubergine 'Violetta Lunga' was red salad onion 'Rossa Lunga di Firenze', beetroot of Chioggia, wild rocket, chicory 'Rossa di Treviso' and borlotti bean 'Lamon'.

As with growing vegetables in pots, after choosing what plants to grow in your bed, you need to decide whether you will raise the vegetables from seed or buy young plants (or use a combination of both). For the biggest selection, grow from seed, but you can also buy ready-grown seedlings, plugs or even larger plants. Garden centres will have a limited range, while a bigger selection can be found at specialist nurseries. Some seeds can be sown directly into the soil during late spring and early summer, but others will need sowing earlier in the year so that you have good-sized vegetables or herbs for planting out later.

Planting out

When the danger of frost has passed, usually in late May in many parts of the United Kingdom, you can start to plant up your bed. First divide the frame into squares. You could do this by marking the surface of the compost mix with a cane, but I prefer something more accurate, so I hammer small nails around the edge and then run strings across to make a grid pattern.

A single plant of a large vegetable, such as tomato, chilli pepper, aubergine and sweet pepper, should be planted at the centre of the square, while I like to ensure a bumper crop of leafy herbs, such as basil, by arranging four plants per square.

Seeds of salad leaves, carrots, beetroot, spring onion, chicory and chard should be sown in short rows, following the instructions on the packet and adding a label to remind you of the variety. Some seeds need a bit more attention lavished on them. For instance, before planting bean seeds, first erect a wigwam of canes for them to climb up. As this will cast shade over other crops in the bed, it is best to place it at the back of the frame. (However, I have put a wigwam in the centre of the bed before and put a shade-tolerant lettuce in the space behind it.) Sow two bean seeds at the base of each cane and remove the weakest of each pair after they are about an inch long. Although they should naturally twine around the canes, you may have to occasionally give them a bit of a helping hand or gently secure them to the support with garden twine.

You will also need to provide small canes to support crops that carry heavy fruit, such as aubergines, chilli peppers, tomatoes and sweet peppers. Do this when plants are about 6 in. (15 cm) and tie in regularly.

After planting, water well and cover bare patches with pieces of galvanized chicken wire. This may look ugly, but it will stop wildlife from foraging and will deter cats from using the raised bed as an alfresco litter tray. It can be removed once the plants are actively growing.

To maintain the bed, hoick out weeds whenever you spot them, water regularly, especially during dry spells, and thin out seed-raised plants so that each has enough room to grow—the distance will depend on the variety and is usually written on the back of the seed packet. Don't consign all of the superfluous seedlings to the compost bin. Some, such as rocket and beetroot, are delicious.

To ensure you get a great crop, feed vegetables that produce fruit once a week with a liquid tomato food after flowers appear. Leafy crops such as salads and herbs need to be picked regularly to produce lots more zingy, tasty growth. This technique works especially well with basil, as by pinching the tips regularly you'll end up with a really bushy plant that will yield lots of leaves. Also, nip off any flower-heads that pop up on plants grown for their leaves, as the flavour will suffer once they start to channel their energy into making seeds.

Adding flowers

If a raised bed dedicated solely to vegetables strikes you as a bit too utilitarian, you can increase its ornamental value with flowers. I have seen beds where each of the

Louis and I prepare plants for the square bed potager.
Photograph by Caroline Hughes.

squares was dedicated to a different bloom, but this look is too chaotic for me, with so many clashing colours and plant shapes. Far easier on the eye is a raised bed potager, based on the traditional French growing system where flowers (some of which can be eaten) are combined with attractive edible plants. To do this, decide what you want to grow and then work out a pattern on paper before transferring it to the bed. There are endless possibilities, but here's a tried and tested recipe for a 3 ft. by 3 ft. (90 cm by 90 cm) bed using ready-grown plants—this bed looked great for about five months and became a real talking point among visitors to my garden.

The ingredients

six runner beans ('Fandango')

four nasturtiums (Tropaeolum majus 'Alaska')

four yellow violas

four marigolds

one courgette

one aubergine

one chilli pepper

one tomato

seven wild rockets

eight lettuces

six 6 ft. garden canes

Left: Arranging vegetables before planting. Photograph by Caroline Hughes.

Right: Popping an aubergine (eggplant) into the corner of the bed. Photograph by Caroline Hughes.

First remove any strings, as you will not be planting into squares, then start by arranging canes in the centre of the bed to make a wigwam, and tie the tops together with garden twine. Plant a runner bean at the base of each, and twine the stem gently around the cane. Starting in a corner, plant one edge of the raised bed in this sequence: viola, lettuce, nasturtium, lettuce and again viola. Repeat the pattern on the opposite side. Fill the two remaining edges with a marigold, nasturtium and another marigold. Add a chilli pepper, aubergine, courgette and tomato, planting behind the lettuce in each corner. Finish by filling any empty spaces with rocket. This speedy salad will provide pickings immediately and will carry on producing leaves for many weeks, until they are eventually crowded out by the other plants.

Watering the bed after planting it. The strip of copper tape around the bed is to repel slugs and snails. Photograph by Caroline Hughes.

4

Taming Monsters

COMMON SENSE TELLS me, as does the occasional garden designer, that I shouldn't really grow towering perennials or plants with mammoth leaves in the garden. Not only are they completely out of scale with the minuscule amount space available to me, but they will completely dominate those plants that are more vertically challenged or that have a more shy and retiring nature.

Well, that may be so, but if I'd always followed the most sensible advice offered to me, I don't think I would have had half as much fun in my life as I have. So, whether or not it's wise, I sometimes throw caution to the wind and grow exactly what I want to in my own garden.

And why shouldn't I? There are far too many fabulous plants available that I want to try, and just because my garden is pint-sized doesn't mean I have to give them all a wide berth. I really would not have enjoyed gardening half as much if I had never taken the opportunity to elbow in the odd bamboo, tree fern, palm or hardy banana, or various lofty grasses and shrubs with leaves so large they resemble a fully unfolded pocket handkerchief.

Of course, growing the giants of the plant world or finding a spot for an unruly beast has to be handled with care. Turn your back for a few weeks and you will find them making a bid for total garden domination, reducing a diverse celebration of plant life into a place of worship for a single plant. However, with clever and regular maintenance, along with a pair of secateurs (pruning shears) and a ball of garden twine, even the most vicious monster can be tamed to work within your space.

Opposite: Tall plants thrive in this small front garden. Photograph by Jonathan Buckley, courtesy of The Garden Collection.

123

Many gardeners avoid large plants in small gardens, but this exotic garden demonstrates how bananas, palms, bamboos and other leafy exotics can work well in a confined space.
Photograph by Jonathan Buckley, courtesy of The Garden Collection.

Bamboozled by bamboo?

Choosing a bamboo for the garden seems to strike fear into the heart of many gardeners. They worry, fairly irrationally in my opinion, about how far these plants will spread and generally talk themselves out of planting them, thinking that once a bamboo is in the ground there's absolutely nothing a gardener can do to halt its advance. Rest assured, waverers, planting a bamboo is not like introducing a pernicious weed into your garden. You will not wake up one morning to discover that your plot now resembles a railway embankment lost under an impenetrable thicket of Japanese knotweed.

I can personally vouch for this. I've grown three in the garden for several years, which have made nice, tight clumps that most certainly haven't outgrown their welcome. There are two specimens of the divine *Phyllostachys nigra*, or black bamboo, and one of *P. aurea*, which admittedly spreads by underground rhizomes, but at a fairly sedate pace that will never catch you out by surprise.

I have long failed to understand why some people consider bamboos a pest or problematic. Anyone armed with a sharp spade can easily remove a wayward

Bamboos are best placed so that you can catch sunlight grazing through the canes.

shoot—it really is not a hardship. I find that my transplanting spade made by Dutch company Sneeboer is ideal. The head of the spade is very narrow, so it can be manipulated around other plants easily without causing damage, and the razor-sharp blade will sever an underground stem with a single strike, quickly putting an end to any fears that the plant will take over.

If you are concerned about bamboos spreading or have a haphazard approach to garden maintenance, choose a clump-forming species rather than those with runners. Some *Phyllostachys*, *Bambusa* and *Chusquea* are ideal, including my favourite, *Phyllostachys nigra*. *Fargesia murielae* 'Simba' looks like a fountain of fresh green foliage and reaches 6 ft. (1.8 m), while *F. robusta* is particularly showy, with emerald green canes up to 13 ft. (4 m) offset by white culm sheaths. *Borinda scabrida* (syn. *Fargesia scabrida*) grows to 10 ft. (3 m) and has slate blue canes that are revealed when the orange culm sheaths drop. If your garden is tiny or you want a bamboo for a pot, try *F. murielae* 'Bimbo'. It is small and beautifully formed, making a mound of 3 ft. (90 cm) stems.

Alternatively, if you are brave enough to plant an invasive bamboo (this includes *Chimonobambusa*, *Pleioblastus* and *Sasa*, along with some varieties of *Arundinaria*, *Clavinodum*, *Hibanobambusa*, *Indocalamus*, *Phyllostachys*, *Pseudosasa*, *Sasaella*, *Semiarundinaria*, *Sinobambusa* and *Yushania*) you can restrict its growth by installing a below-ground barrier. Paving slabs, pre-cast concrete drain sections and root barrier fabrics are perfect, but avoid butyl pond liners as the tapered point of a runner can easily pierce its way through. The barrier should be at least 2 ft. (60 cm) deep and ideally 4 ft. (1.2 m)—ensure that it protrudes 3 in. (8 cm) above the soil line to prevent rhizomes escaping over the top of the barrier. If you use a fabric barrier, make sure that the ends of the material overlap by about a foot and secure them with appropriate glue.

Apart from keeping bamboos within bounds by removing canes that grow where I don't want them to, I like to prune my bamboos creatively. Both of the varieties in my garden have showy stems, but the flush of new, leafy growth every year means they are hidden by masses of green foliage. To reveal the canes, I strip the leaves from the bottom third of them. With some varieties you can simply do this by taking the side branch firmly with your thumb and forefinger, and then snapping it downwards with a sharp movement. If the branches don't snap off cleanly, you will have to resort to cutting them off, flush with the cane.

Once you have stripped the stems you could try something that I have been told professional growers do when preparing their plants for flower shows: polish each individual stem with a soft cloth moistened with vegetable oil. This apparently keeps bamboos looking their best, but for lack of time and about a hundred other reasons I have not tried this out for myself.

After clearing the stems I reduce congestion inside the clump by pruning to the ground any thin, spindly or dying canes. This makes the bamboo far more attractive, and a bit of daylight through the clump means that individual canes have a chance to be seen at their best. Thinning out is not just for cosmetic reasons, however; it also allows space for new canes to grow with a bit of elbow room.

Not all creative pruning techniques work aesthetically. I once visited Pinsla Garden in Cornwall, a magical space that the owners use as an outdoor gallery for their works of art. I have to emphasize that I really like this garden, but the owners prune many of their plants, and they have even rounded off several clumps of bamboo to echo the shape of some evergreen shrubs that have been clipped into domes. To me bamboos are beautiful in their natural state, and they rarely make even clumps. The unified shapes they had been clipped into did not suit them—they seemed to have lost all of their natural grace when the teeth of the hedge trimmer bit into their canes.

That's not to say I don't try to restrain my bamboos. I sometimes have to. Plants are often buffeted by strong gusts of wind in my garden, and a clump of bamboo has developed a pronounced slant towards the path that runs down the middle of the plot. If a branch develops too much of a bend and falls awkwardly across the path, I

Black bamboo (*Phyllostachys nigra*) is prevented from spilling out all over the path with a tie across its belly.

have found that it often springs back to a more upright position if the top is pruned slightly to remove some of the weight. Take care when doing this. If you remove only the tips or cut above head height, nobody will notice, but if you remove a large portion of the stem you'll be left with an ugly stump that everybody will see. If reducing the bulk of canes has no effect, you might have to resort to simply removing the offending branch by cutting it off completely flush with the ground.

If a clump grows too close to the path and the canes stymie access by flopping in the way, it may be necessary to curb the entire plant with the horticultural equivalent of a gastric band. To do this, I hammer a short tree stake behind each clump, ensuring that it is placed where it can't be seen. Then I attach a length of brown flexible tubing to it, before wrapping it around the plant to make a large ring, pulling it as tight as possible and then tying the other end to the stake. Bamboos with a substantial girth may need two or even three bands of tubing around them to keep them under control. The brown tubing is ideal, because it's almost unnoticeable against dark-stemmed bamboos, and it is soon hidden by foliage anyway, giving the clump an attractive, taut silhouette with no saggy bits (you see, I said the effect was similar to a gastric band).

For a more attractive look, where you can blatantly see the restraints, or to prevent very large clumps from spilling out, you can use rope. I've seen this work effectively in several gardens, although there's more than a little resemblance to the tasselled rope tiebacks that Granny and Granddad Cox used to tether their heavy gold velvet drapes during the 1970s.

Disasters

Not all giant plants are easily tamed. Like many plantaholics, I have a habit of falling in love with enormous plants I see in larger gardens and then returning home thinking I must try to find a way to grow them in mine. Among those that have won my heart is *Impatiens tinctoria*, a mammoth perennial that held court in the part woodland, part stream garden of Trengwainton, near Penzance in Cornwall. It's a real beauty that spreads quickly in moist soil to form big clumps of fleshy stems, up to 6 ft. (1.8 m), which are topped with sprays of scented white flowers. I made it my mission to find a specimen and eventually tracked it down, squeezing it into a gap in a bed where I thought I'd be able to curb its enthusiasm with a few deft snips whenever necessary. Oh how wrong I was. Its height wasn't a problem, as it was grown at the foot of a fence, but it wanted to sprawl out. Unfortunately, removing the spreading stems left it looking rather weedy and not at all like the handsome plant I had seen at Trengwainton. After a season of growing it, I served it with an eviction notice.

Impatiens tinctoria has lovely white flowers but is too much of a thug in a small space.

Apart from other people's gardens, perhaps the greatest influence on my plant buying is the wonderful two-volume *Conservatory and Indoor Plants* by Roger Phillips and Martyn Rix. When I first found my copy, in a second-hand bookshop, I was passionate about creating an exotic garden similar in style to that created by the late Christopher Lloyd at Great Dixter. Following his lead, I wanted to include vibrant-coloured dahlias in my planting scheme and was growing varieties such as *Dahlia* 'Pink Giraffe', which has zany pink-and-white-striped petals. My interest in these plants led me to look them up in *Conservatory and Indoor Plants*, and my jaw almost hit the ground when I turned to page 218 and saw a picture of *D. imperialis*, the aptly named tree dahlia. The specimen dwarfed a group of children in Mexico, and I decided on the spot that I had to grow it, even though the description made it clear that it could eventually reach 30 ft. (9 m) tall.

A telephone call to Winchester Growers, holders of the UK's National Dahlia Collection, resulted in a rooted cutting being sent to me. It was about the size of pencil when it arrived in a little box, so I potted it up into a 3 in. pot. It quickly outgrew this and a few weeks later was moved up into a 6 in. pot. Potting it up after this point became a regular job, until early summer when I took the plunge and planted it out. Within weeks it was towering above me, and the wide, graceful spread of its branches completely obscured the back of my garden from the windows of my house.

Everybody who visited commented on this unusual perennial, and I truly admired its architectural shape. However, I never got to enjoy its striking pink flowers that crown the top of the plant in warmer climates. It needs a very long, warm season, and this is something that I could not provide in my garden (can any in the United Kingdom?). Unfortunately, after a sharp frost in November, I opened the curtains and was met by a gruesome sight. The dahlia had turned jet black overnight, and the stems gradually turned to a mushy pile on the ground over the next week or so. With heavy heart I later dug up the clump, and I have never grown it again.

On another occasion I decided rashly to grow Spanish reed (*Arundo donax*). I had seen this plant many times in subtropical gardens and admired the stately stands of thick, glaucous stems. In my mind, planting one of these would give my garden instantaneous exotic credentials, so I was delighted when I spotted a specimen for sale while visiting Spinners Garden and Nursery in the New Forest, Hampshire. I returned home with a 1/2-gallon (2-litre) pot in the boot of my car and planted it exactly where the dahlia had previously grown.

The arundo was a sneaky plant, a bit like one of those friendly-looking dogs that you have to stroke but that will bite you as soon as you turn your back. One minute the plant was crawling along, leaving me wondering if it would ever grow,

The final cut: an imposing clump of *Arundo donax* is cut down before removal from the garden. Photograph by Alison Reid.

Arundo donax is an impressive plant, but its towering stems and spreading habit are not ideal in a small garden. This specimen's tenure in my garden was short but sweet.

and the next it was making a bolt for the sky. It easily reached 15 ft. (4.6 m) and spread quickly to make a hefty clump, elbowing lesser plants out of the way with its rhizomes, which started to pop up everywhere, mainly where I didn't want them.

Again, many people admired it, but my partner could not stand it, and I eventually had to admit that it was too thuggish even for me. Armed with a spade, I spent an hour or so digging the main clump from the soil and trying to remove all the runners—a task at which I failed, as new stems kept appearing for several months afterwards. Evicting such an impressive plant was done with a heavy heart, so I offered some rooted shoots to a neighbour. As I write, I can see it rising above his fence and can't help wondering how long it will be before it's moved on again.

Dwarfing

There's no way that I'd recommend planting giant rhubarb (*Gunnera manicata*), which grows up to 8 ft. (2.4 m) tall with a spread of 12 ft. (3.6 m) or more, in a small garden. But many plant lovers are an adventurous breed who often ignore the rules and grow the plants that really turn them on, whether they have room for them or not.

To keep gunnera in a pot, you will have to feed and water it often.

A few years ago when I visited the tiny garden at 28 Kensington Road in Bristol, near the west coast of England, it was the smallest garden open for the National Gardens Scheme charity. The urban plot was only 20 ft. by 18 ft., but owners Grenville Johnson and Alan Elms had managed to squeeze in hundreds of plants, including a gunnera.

Rather than sink the gunnera into the soil, they grew it in a large pot, where it was doing very well. According to the couple, it needed copious watering and feeding to keep in good shape, and it produced a canopy of leaves that never really got out of control. The restriction of the pot obviously had a natural dwarfing effect on the plant, and if any leaves outgrew their welcome, they were simply snipped off. Surely proof that the saying 'You can't have your cake and eat it too' is not always accurate.

From the upstairs back window of my house I can see a wonderful loquat (*Eriobotrya japonica*) in a neighbour's garden that must be about 25 ft. (7.6 m) tall and 15 ft. (4.6 m) wide. This lovely specimen fruits freely in the blessed micro-climate found in London and would do so in sheltered spots within other cities with a temperate climate. However, it has also grown very large and is not ideal for a garden the same size as mine. So what can you do if you love those long, corrugated green leaves as much as I do? The answer: grow it in a pot. I have taken the sensible decision to restrict the growth of mine by planting it in a large terrazzo cube. It does very well, and I have grown it as a standard, removing all the lower leaves and branches, and pinching back the upper shoots to create a bushy head.

Apart from its good looks, the loquat is a very forgiving plant. Impatient new shoots are regularly knocked back by a late frost, so I have to prune off the browning foliage—happily, this results in a flush of new leaves down the stems.

Another giant that grows well, but whose growth is restrained by plunging into a container, is the honey bush, *Melianthus major*. An irresistible plant with jag-

Honey bush (*Melianthus major*) is a big, untidy shrub for a small garden, but in a pot it makes a neatish hummock of glaucous foliage.

ged, greyish blue leaves that smell like crunchy peanut butter when crushed or brushed past, it started at the back of a bed, where it soon began to encroach on just about everything around it. I was forced into cutting off stems regularly, which worked to a degree, but it was still too big and bulky, and the stems lazily flopped onto smaller plants. Eventually I took the plunge and hoicked it out of the ground. It's not a plant I would discard or want to give away, so I planted it into a 15 in. pot. This has had the desired effect, resulting in a plant that produces a rounded mound of foliage that is never antisocial or in need of regular maintenance.

When choosing plants for containers, you need to consider carefully the amount of free room you have and the requirements of the specimens you want to grow. If you are really starved of space, your aim should not be to introduce a plant that needs a pot with the diameter of a child's swimming pool—this will only mean you'll end up losing so much valuable living space on a patio or deck.

Ideally go for something that is compact, fastigiate (upright, narrowing towards the top), that can be muzzled by pruning or that can be grown as a standard with a head of leaves that won't take up too much of your garden's living space. Upright birches such as *Betula nigra* will provide a contemporary woodland feel, while venerable olives or mature grapevines will add a touch of the Mediterranean. Many large shrubs are perfect, such as heavenly bamboo (*Nandina domestica*) and most Japanese maples. Topiary and plants that need regularly clipping are ideal, as they are mechanically prevented from outgrowing their allotted space. Box, bay, junipers, hollies and ligustrum are just some of the plants you could consider.

I've long admired the large primrose yellow flowers and evergreen leaves of *Magnolia grandiflora*, which are often seen draped across the sunny facade of a stately home. Now there's no way I'm going to suggest you grow a plant that can get up to 60 ft. (18 m) tall in a pot when you only have a few feet to spare, but you could go for the next best thing—a dwarf version. *Magnolia grandiflora* 'Little Gem' will eventually reach 20 ft. (6 m) in ideal conditions but is unlikely to reach this if restricted to a container. With a narrow columnar habit, oval leaves and smaller flowers, it can hardly be described as similar to its towering relation, but it does at least capture its spirit. (In a similar vein, but at a complete tangent from containers, I also like to capture the essence of larger plants by growing closely related smaller ones. A good example is *Gunnera magellanica*. Rather than trying to grow *G. manicata* in a pot, I bought this ground-hugging Chilean variety and planted it on the edge of my patio, where it flourishes in a damp, shady spot. It's a real marvel that only grows a few inches tall, but its leaves and flowers are the perfect miniature replicas of the giant rhubarb.)

Not all big plants respond well to container culture. I bought a honey spurge (*Euphorbia mellifera*) at the same time as my mother-in-law. Mine went straight into

Related to the giant rhubarb, *Gunnera magellanica* spreads at the foot of a silvery astelia. The plant alongside is *Saxifraga* 'Cotton Crochet'.

Honey spurge (*Euphorbia mellifera*) will sulk in a pot but needs careful pruning to keep it under control in a small garden.

the ground and hers into a 12 in. pot. As there is a lot of rivalry between us, I'm delighted to say that mine is about 6 ft. (1.8 m) tall with a similar spread and is smothered with dozens of the heady, honey-scented flower-heads in late spring. Sadly, hers has about four weedy stems topped with pitiful flower-heads.

Most of my large plants grow in pots filled with a loam-based compost containing fertilizer and a fair amount of horticultural grit to improve drainage. The compost is also fairly good at retaining water and is somewhat heavy, perfect for plants with a lot of top growth as it offers some stability to prevent them being blown over by a strong gust of wind.

To ensure plants remain at their best, you will need to start feeding them after about three months when the fertilizer starts to run out. During the year I use a general liquid fertilizer, then in spring push a plug of controlled-release fertilizer into the top of pots. Apart from this, they just need watering with great regularity.

In cold or exposed gardens, plants in pots will need protecting over winter, as the roots growing near the edges are vulnerable to freezing temperatures. If the plant isn't that big and there is room in a greenhouse, shed or other frost-free place, you could try moving it there. If not, move it to a more sheltered or warmer part of the garden, such as close to the walls of the house, then wrap the container with bubble wrap or hessian (burlap) held securely in place with twine. A good idea passed on to me by Christine Shaw, manager of the excellent Architectural Plants nursery in Chichester, West Sussex, is to line the inside of pots with bubble wrap before planting, which negates the need to wrap plants up in winter. Clever.

Aquatics in a tub

Whenever I see a water feature in a garden, whether it's a pool, natural stream, rill or plunging waterfall, I move towards it as if pulled by an invisible cord. I guess it must be one of those primeval things, the same kind of irresistible urge that attracts us to the flickering flames of a campfire, or the reason why men (and it is only men) congregate around the smoky coals of a barbecue.

If I could create my dream water feature, it would be a meandering stream that flows into a natural-looking pond with a substantial bog garden at its edge. It would be incredibly well stocked. Among the marginal plants might be North American yellow skunk cabbage (*Lysichiton americanus*), *Calla palustris*, lesser reed mace (*Typha angustifolia*), arum lily and a cavalcade of irises, including the many varieties of *Iris laevigata*, *I. pseudacorus* and *I. versicolor*. It would be filled with the jewel-like flowers of water lilies, and the bog would be a close-knit tapestry of *Rheum palmatum*, *Carex elata* 'Aurea', *Astilbe*, *Darmera peltata*, *Gunnera* and candelabra primulas such as *Primula beesiana* and *P. pulverulenta*. Ah well, while I live in East London this will have to remain a dream for the future, but it is still possible to grow water-loving plants in the garden, as long as you think small.

Although you could hive off part of your space and build a small pond, you can easily satisfy your desire for growing water-loving plants by using a half wooden barrel. These are generally 3 ft. across and are widely available from garden centres. There's no need to line the inside with butyl or plastic, as these barrels are a by-product of the whisky industry and are completely watertight. (If you're lucky you may even get a whiff of the 'water of life'.) When buying, look for used vessels and avoid new reproductions, which don't look as good and may develop leaks. The name of the distillery should be stamped on the outside, and the inside should be slightly charred, a technique used by barrel manufacturers to add flavour to the spirits.

Aquatic plants will thrive if they receive sunlight, so avoid placing your barrel in an area that receives heavy shade throughout summer. A partially shady spot is ideal, as too much sun can promote the growth of algae, while too much shade will result in low oxygen levels in your pond.

Plants are essential to prevent algae, which spreads rapidly in sunlight and prospers when nutrients are created by mineral salts in the water, thereby polluting and colouring the pond. Surface-covering plants will provide shade for the water and help to limit the development of algae by taking up the nutrients.

Start off your pond by filling the barrel with water, leaving a gap of about 2 in. from the surface of the water to the lip of the pot. Now treat it like any other pond, and plant it up with a selection of marginal, oxygenating and floating aquatic plants. Creating shelves for marginal plants is easy: simply stand them on some upturned pots or bricks submerged along the inside edge of the barrel.

Although you could choose to grow some vigorous aquatics, you are better off choosing plants that are better behaved. This way you'll avoid ending up with a big barrel of foliage with hardly a chink of water showing.

For me, choosing marginals is a bit like being a child in a toy shop—there are so many wonderful plants to choose from. A must for foliage is *Typha minima*, a graceful miniature bulrush that only grows to 24 in. (60 cm) with slender spikes of brown flowers. The horsetail, *Equisetum arvense*, grows to 12 in. (30 cm) and has head-turning green stems emblazoned with black bands. In normal situations it is invasive, but not when contained in a pot. With its wire-like, tightly coiled green leaves, *Juncus inflexus* 'Afro' is perfectly named and a choice rush for barrels. There are other rushes with similar corkscrew leaves that are worth growing, such as *J. decipiens* 'Curly-wurly' and *J. decipiens* 'Spiralis Nana'. Japanese rush, *Acorus gramineus*, is a showy plant for barrels. There are many varieties, but 'Ogon' stands out for its yellow and green vertically striped leaves.

There's no point having a barrel container and only filling it with foliage marginals, so include a few flowers. *Butomus umbellatus* is a lovely British native with 3 ft. (90 cm) stems that explode with umbels of pink flowers, while *Sagittaria sagittifolia* has lovely, arrow-shaped, green leaves that form a 2 ft. (60 cm) tall nest for slender spikes of pretty white flowers in summer. Another favourite of mine is *Myosotis scorpioides*, otherwise known as water forget-me-not, which is smothered in tiny, sky blue flowers in early summer.

You can barely see submerged plants, but they are essential for oxygenating the water. A good choice is whorled milfoil (*Myriophyllum verticillatum*) or hair grass (*Eleocharis acicularis*). There are many invasive submerged aquatics that escape from garden ponds and that are responsible for choking our waterways, outcompeting native plants and impacting on local populations of wildlife. Sadly, many irresponsible garden centres and aquatic nurseries continue to sell these plants, so do your bit and avoid them at all costs. This is not an exhaustive list, but invasive plants to shun include curly waterweed (*Lagarosiphon major*), Canadian pondweed (*Elodea canadensis*) and parrot's feather (*Myriophyllum aquaticum*).

The real divas of any pond are water lilies, and while a large proportion of the family need plenty of room to thrive, dwarf and pygmy water lilies are perfect in water only 6 in. (15 cm) to 1^1/$_2$ ft. (45 cm) deep. *Nymphaea* 'Aurora' has cup-shaped yellow flowers that age dramatically, turning from orange to red. *Nymphaea* 'Joanne Pring' (syn. *N. tetragona* 'Johann Pring') has pink, star-shaped flowers, and *N. tetragona* 'Alba' is one of the smallest water lilies around, with each white bloom only an inch across.

As it's only a fraction the size of an in-ground pond, a barrel water feature is a breeze to care for. If it takes any more than a glance or a few minutes a week, you're doing something wrong. Like any other pond, you will need to top up the water level if it starts to drop during a spell of hot weather. And to prevent the water from being discoloured, trim off any dead or dying leaves, along with any dead flower-heads.

Training

There's nothing new about training shrubs against walls or fences. These structures have long been used to support large plants with rather lax growth. You could visit thousands of plots and find pyracanthas, ceanothus, jasmine, camellia, chaenomeles, *Viburnum rhytidophyllum* and countless other plants tied to a series of horizontal wires, where they are pruned regularly to prevent them from outgrowing their allotted space. But in a small garden, where you may only have room for one or two

Usually grown as a free-standing bush, bottlebrush (*Callistemon*) is perfectly happy trained on wires against a fence or wall.

wall shrubs, you would be out of your mind to pick such ordinary shrubs as these when there are more exciting plants to grow.

If you have a warm, sheltered and sunny garden you could grow showy bougainvillea against a wall, but this plant is frost tender, so if you can't provide the right conditions it is best grown in a large pot. Insert a piece of trellis into the same container or make a frame out of stout canes lashed together with twine, and train the branches against it. Once the frame is filled, snip off any branches that you don't need. The bougainvillea can have a summer holiday outside and can be transported to a frost-free place from autumn onwards.

Bottlebrushes are choice shrubs that have amazing flowers in many different colours. They are lovely when grown free-standing, but their shape is messy, especially those with arching branches. Many, many years ago I looked after the glasshouses for a horticultural college and grew a bottlebrush on a piece of trellis that had been pushed up against the sides of a greenhouse to provide a screen. I transferred this method to my own garden and grew *Callistemon citrinus* 'Splendens' in a 5.5-gallon (25-litre) pot up against some canes arranged in a fan shape. The plant soon covered the cane, and other branches were manipulated until you could barely see daylight through it. Sadly, my burgeoning collection of plants meant I had to downsize, and I made the tough decision to give the bottlebrush away.

When it's in full bloom, *Fremontodendron* 'California Glory' creates a memorable spectacle in the garden. The large, yellow, cup-shaped flowers are borne prolifically over summer and into autumn, and plants are extremely drought tolerant when established. It is ideal against a wall and can be kept in order by pruning after flowering.

I love the sweet-scented yellow flowers of *Cytisus battandieri* (pineapple broom), but its open, sprawling habit of growth makes it a plant to avoid growing as a freestanding shrub. However, grow it against a wall and you'll find it behaves itself impeccably. Another favourite shrub to try is *Acacia pravissima* (oven's wattle). The pendulous branches are clad with distinctive triangular leaves and smothered with tiny yellow mimosa flowers in spring.

5
Seasonal Stars

MY GARDEN IS a bit like a long-running soap opera. There are a few 'non-speaking' characters that barely change from one month to the next but that are essential to give the garden continuity. This includes evergreen ivies, ×*Fatshedera lizei* and other plants that have the important role of camouflaging my fences and that will always remain in the background. Then there is the regular cast: plants that play a pivotal part in the look of my garden and are always there. They don't always have something to say, but they may have several storylines a year—when in flower or fruit, or when the fading blooms turn to long-lasting, sculptural seed heads.

Although this cast works well, knitting together perfectly and providing interest all year round, I'm the writer and producer of this show, and I like to stir things up occasionally by introducing a star whose role is fleeting but dramatic and memorable. I am, of course, describing bulbs and annuals.

Some of these might be new plants, started from seed or snapped up on impulse in the garden centre, while others are returning characters, plants that remain beneath ground for much of the year, or stowed away in pots in the greenhouse, until they are ready to flower—then it is time for them to grab all the glory and be given a major storyline. (Much to the disgruntlement of the regulars, I imagine.)

Plants that only make a brief appearance are valuable in a small garden. At the height of summer, tender annuals can be bought to plug any gaps in beds or to fill hanging baskets, and groups of them can be arranged in pots on a hard surface to create a multi-layered, three-dimensional display. This can be a useful way to make

Opposite: Dwarf formosa lily (*Lilium formosanum* var. *pricei*) spreads quickly to fill a pot and has powerfully scented flowers.

143

a drab corner more alluring or to disguise an ugly feature, such as the bay where you might store your rubbish bins.

Most bulbs do not compete with perennials or shrubs for space in the garden, but they usually complement them whenever they appear, creating pleasing combinations as they erupt from the ground. The fact that they lay hidden below the surface for much of the year means you can squeeze many more plants into your garden, without hiving off space from your beds.

As with plants for beds and borders, bulbs should be chosen carefully to ensure they complement the rest of your planting scheme. This is most important with summer bulbs, as they will be sharing the garden or even rubbing shoulders with flowering perennials. If they are out of scale with neighbouring plants or the colours clash horribly, the effect won't flatter your garden at all and is likely to cause great irritation—at least for a few weeks. Taking the permanent planting scheme into consideration isn't as important for early spring flowers, as they will likely have much of the garden to themselves. If you plant these bulbs, why not look upon it as an opportunity to grow flowers with completely different colours to those of the perennials and shrubs that appear in a few months' time?

In my garden I grow a combination of spring-, summer- and autumn-flowering bulbs that have been planted in the ground, and some summer-flowering bulbs that permanently reside in pots. The potted bulbs are brought out of the greenhouse and put in prominent spots, on the patio, deck or to plug a hole in a bed when they are in flower. As soon as they start to fade, it's time for them to go back into the greenhouse. Job done.

Early spring bulbs

After winter, which always seems to drag on and on, nothing lifts my spirits more than seeing the fresh emerald foliage of daffodils and snowdrops emerging from the bare earth. The growth from these bundles of stored energy is unstoppable, and I know that in a matter of weeks I will be enjoying their beautiful flowers. For me, their leaves breaking through the surface of the soil marks the demise of the dark nights and a welcome return to spring.

Daffodils and snowdrops are the only bulbs that I grow in my back garden. Largely this is due to space, as too many different bulbs thrown together in such confined quarters would look chaotic, like a spilt bag of dolly mixture sweets. But it is also because I prefer the impact of flowers grown en masse—individually, you might have to stoop, crawl or generally prostrate yourself at the feet of a flower to enjoy it, but plant a crowd of flowers and you can marvel at them from a distance.

This is a useful trick that allows everybody in my household a chance to see the flowers. The children don't always want to go outdoors, especially when it is chilly, but they can still enjoy the burst of colour from the upstairs windows of the house.

By late winter the daffodils have risen well above the stubby clumps of perennials that have been cut back or the crowns of plants that are about to stir into life. I grow only *Narcissus* 'Tête-à-tête', a dwarf variety that generally grows to about 8 in. (20 cm). It's an excellent plant with two or three buttercup yellow flowers per stem that appear between February and March.

Providing a carpet of white beneath the daffodils is a random assortment of snowdrops. I've absolutely no idea what variety they are, and would probably need to call in a dedicated galanthophile equipped with magnifying glass and kneepads to help me identify them. Although I don't know their names, I do know they have impeccable ancestry. I picked them up 'in the green' after visiting The Gardens of Easton Lodge in Essex, a crumbling, romantic garden that is undergoing serious restoration after many years of neglect. Designed by Harold Peto in 1902, the gardens are a mecca for snowdrop lovers, and I have visited many times to see the sheets of white that spread beneath deciduous trees. Each year the garden staff lift, divide and replant some of the clumps after flowering, but also offer some for sale. One

Narcissus 'Tête-à-tête' flowering in my sleeper bed in early spring.

Delicate snowdrops can't really be appreciated from a distance. To give them close attention you will need to get down on your hands and knees.

time I was lucky enough to be looking around the garden after they had lifted the bulbs and came away with two mixed bags of snowdrops of about a hundred plants in total.

Although the white snowdrops complement the yellow of the daffodils, providing lots of cheery colour, I do want the scheme to have a little more pizzazz. In the future I will add blue *Iris reticulata*, which flowers at the same time. At about 6 in. (15 cm) tall, it would allow a good graduation of height between the snowdrop and the taller daffodils.

While simplicity rules in the back garden, I do grow more bulbs in the front. This is for one main reason. As we spend quite a lot of time in our snug lounge over winter and early spring, I felt it was important that the front garden, which we look directly out on from the comfort of our couch, have plenty of interesting treasures in it for us all to admire. Not only that, but it gives me a boost when I walk down the front path past lots of colour and not just past plants that are still in a state of hibernation.

I have gone for white and yellow bulbs in the front, which illuminate this gloomy patch like an outdoor light bulb and work well with the permanent plants. Most of these are green, but there's also a large stand of *Luzula sylvatica* 'Aurea', a woodrush that is at its best at this time of year, with acid yellow leaves, and a few feet away a group of *Milium effusum* 'Aureum', or Bowles' golden grass, whose strap-like foliage glows a golden yellow in spring.

In a tiny planting pocket occupied by a fern, *Polystichum setiferum*, I've planted a group of *Brimeura amethystina* 'Alba', which make a pretty white skirt around the fern's feathery fronds in May. Growing up to 8 in. (20 cm), this bulb looks like a miniature bluebell, with tubular flowers held on slender stalks. The species is also well worth growing and has blue flowers.

In the main bed, the first to flower are two small groups of winter aconites that grow close to the path. The egg yolk yellow flowers of *Eranthis cilicica* sometimes appear as early as January and perch on top of a nest of bronze-tinged foliage. As this plant only grows to 2 in. (5 cm) tall, you need to give it a prominent position. Almost echoing the shape of the flowers, in another part of the bed is a group of *Hacquetia epipactis*. This low-growing, clump-forming perennial has tiny yellow flowers fused between green bracts that appear during late winter and early spring.

Things really start to motor from February, when *Narcissus* 'February Gold' flowers. Planted randomly in the bed, this dwarf cyclamineus type grows to about 12 in. (30 cm) and has gorgeous golden trumpets that continue into March. Interest at ground level is provided by three small groups of *Crocus chrysanthus* 'Snow Bunting', a choice little plant with white flowers marked with delicate indigo feathering on the outer petals. In the centre of each flower is a lovely and very noticeable orange stigma.

By April all of the early bulbs have finished, but there is a group of dog's-tooth violets, *Erythronium californicum* 'White Beauty', in the middle of the bed, whose delectable large white flowers are part of a crescendo of spring blooming in the front. This is the bed's moment of glory, with sprays of white froth erupting from a clump of *Brunnera macrophylla* 'Betty Bowring' and delicate snowy flowers rising on wiry stems above leafy woodlander *Epimedium ×youngianum* 'Niveum'. Arching over the path are the leafy stalks of false Solomon's seal, *Maianthemum racemosum*, which terminate in a plume of white, slightly scented flowers.

Autumn bulbs

Most gardeners do not think twice about planting spring- or summer-flowering bulbs, but very few seem to plant bulbs that perk up the garden later in the year. I'm not really sure why this is, but I have a theory. Gardening magazines have special supplements or extra-long features to encourage readers to plant bulbs for spring and summer, but rarely give much coverage to planting bulbs for later in the year. So at the time of year when autumn bulbs need planting, from late summer to early autumn, most gardeners are busily ordering and then planting spring bulbs.

Well, that's my hypothesis anyway, but whatever the real reason, I can't help but think that a lot of people are missing out on growing some wonderful plants. Among those that will hold their own among the fiery tints that embellish autumnal shrubs are the stately *Amaryllis belladonna*, nerines and crinums, all of which are ideal for growing in containers and can be whipped out of the greenhouse when they are about to come into flower.

But size isn't everything, and I'm equally bowled over by much more diminutive bulbs, such as the various yellow sternbergias, autumn-flowering crocus and *Scilla autumnalis*. Perhaps the most celebrated autumn bulbs are cyclamens, and although a small garden is not the place to establish a large, showy carpet of these flowers, you could still plant a few under a tree, at the base of a wall, in a rock garden or at the front of a border. There are many to choose from. *Cyclamen hederifolium* is probably the easiest to grow and has highly decorative leaves with intricate patterns that look like they have been created by an artist practised in sgraffito. *Cyclamen graecum* is found in southern Turkey, along with some Mediterranean islands, and thrives in sun. If you have shady areas, try sweetly scented *C. cyprium*, and *C. cilicium* is a good choice for dry soil, whether at the foot of a wall or base of a hedge.

In my garden I grow five types of *Colchicum*, sometimes misleadingly sold as autumn crocus. These are great value bulbs that do best if they get sun for a few hours each day. I have some in shade and they still flower, but the blooms are not as long lasting and tend to flop quite easily.

In spring the colchicums make a mass of lush, upright foliage that perfectly fills any gaps among perennials that have yet to reach full size. The leaves are quite broad and ribbed like a hosta, and as with a hosta they eventually succumb to the jaws of slugs and snails, before yellowing and completely dying back beneath the soil by early summer.

The flowers appear on naked stems, 6–8 in. (15–20 cm) high, without a sign of foliage, during September and October. Mine are all different shades of pink (white flowers are also available), but there is great variation in shape. *Colchicum autumnale* has soft mauve flowers similar to a crocus, while *C. speciosum* var. *bornmuelleri* has large, violet flowers. *Colchicum cilicicum* has starry, rose-pink flowers on slender stalks, *C. speciosum* has purplish goblets and *C. byzantinum* has open, rosy lilac flowers.

While these are all choice varieties, none are as flamboyant as *Colchicum* 'Waterlily', a head-turning bulb with rosy lilac double flowers. Unfortunately, I don't grow it, but a friend of mine does, in a planter attached to the top of his front garden wall. It's the perfect position. Sometimes the flowers can be lost under the foliage, and you only notice them before they are about to go over. But when the plant is

The fleshy leaves of autumn crocus appear in spring before dying back.

The delicate pink flowers of an autumn crocus bloom beneath the strappy leaf of *Kniphofia northiae*.

grown at chest height, you never miss its flowers, and you certainly won't have to bend or bow to enjoy their good looks.

Summer bulbs

Although there are exceptions (notably tulips), most spring bulbs are subdued when compared to their summer-flowering cousins. Lilies, dahlias, cannas and the rest of this vibrant crowd are like those loud, attention-seeking people you meet at parties, who invariably, due to being so noisy, get all the recognition they had hoped to achieve. But summer bulbs are not party poopers, far from it. These are bulbs you will look forward to see year after year.

'Summer bulbs' is a bit of a loose term, as it includes plants that flower in June, July and August as well as those that start in late summer and continue well into autumn, such as dahlias, cannas, pineapple lilies (*Eucomis*), tiger flowers (*Tigridia*) and *Schizostylis*. In my garden I have planted a few of these permanently in the beds, but I grow more in pots that I wheel out in bud, a week or so before they look like

Intriguing flowers and eye-catching leaves of *Arisaema costatum*.

they might flower. At this time they either grace a sunny spot on the deck or patio, or are squeezed into a gap within the border. I generally don't plunge pots into the soil but disguise them by manipulating a branch or a few leaves of any neighbouring plants. To avoid making an ordeal out of hiding pots, plant bulbs in black containers that will instantly recede into the undergrowth—choose a faux terracotta plastic pot and it will stand out like a beacon.

The earliest bulb to flower in my garden is *Allium cristophii*. In June the papery skin that protects the flower splits open to reveal lots of starry, metallic pink flowers fused onto long, slender filaments. These are tightly bunched together but soon unfurl until you are left with a rounded flower-head that measures about 8 in. (20 cm) across. Mine grows beneath *Thalictrum delavayi* 'Hewitt's Double'. The heads of the allium emerge on 24 in. (60 cm) stalks through the wiry foliage of the thalictrum, whose own foamy pink flowers will burst open a few weeks later. Although this allium is the first summer bulb to flower for me, its presence is felt for a long time. As the blooms fade, you are left with fabulous bronze seed heads that stand up to weathering extremely well, and their skeletal shapes often maintain interest well into winter. Although I like to leave them in place, I have collected the seed heads in

After *Allium cristophii* has finished flowering, the sculptural seed heads can remain well into winter.

the past. They make snazzy decorations at Christmas when attached with thread to the bare branches of my *Cercis canadensis* 'Forest Pansy'.

I love lilies, even the very brash ones that seem to be quite unfashionable at the moment, but I don't have any room in the soil left to plant any. I get around this problem by growing them in pots. I always have a few towering regal lilies, planted mainly for their scent, but am smitten by a plant at the other end of the growth scale. *Lilium formosanum* var. *pricei* (dwarf formosa lily) is often sold as a rock garden plant but is splendid in a terracotta 'long-tom' (tall, narrow) pot. It multiplies quickly in a pot, and within a couple of years you will have lots of 18 in. (45 cm) stems that hold

Eucomis are ideal summer bulbs for planting in pots.

massive white trumpets in early summer. Each nodding flower is flushed with purple on the reverse of the petals and is packed with a typical lily perfume.

If forced to name my favourite summer bulb, I would have to go with the pineapple lily (*Eucomis*). I've been an admirer of this exotic tribe from South Africa for many years and have five different varieties in the garden.

They are real sun worshippers and like moisture-retentive, well-drained soil. If you can't provide this, simply grow them in a large pot. What they can't tolerate is deep shade, in which case they'll produce masses and masses of strappy leaves that soon turn into a floppy mess, without a single flower in sight.

My favourite for its colour and robust constitution is *Eucomis comosa* 'Sparkling Burgundy'. It is a striking plant with a rosette of dark purple leaves that seem much more succulent than others. In late summer a neat flower spike, 60 cm tall, sits in the middle of the foliage, made up of hundreds of tiny, star-shaped, purple flowers beneath a tuft of bronze bracts. Other notable varieties that I grow include *E. comosa*, which makes a rosette of slight wavy leaves and boasts a big spike of white flowers, and *E. bicolor* 'Alba', whose yellowy green flowers are borne on quite slender spikes. I also grow another eucomis that I was given and can't identify. It produces a very large rosette of foliage with 12 in. (30 cm) leaves that are speckled at the base. The 18 in. (45 cm) flower spike is burly. It, too, is speckled below, and the white flowers are marked with a purple centre. Please, if you know what it is, put me out of my misery and let me know.

There's another pineapple lily that I haven't yet grown myself but am dying to get my hands on: *Eucomis vandermerwei* 'Octopus'. I first saw it in the garden of a couple I was interviewing. It was a lovely little thing, perfect for the tiniest of spaces. Its slender leaves were heavily speckled chocolate brown, and its 6 in. (15 cm) spike of maroon flowers was capped by a mottled top knot of bracts.

Unfortunately, eucomis are not entirely hardy and do need some protection to ensure they make it through the winter. If you have them in pots, all you need to do is move them to a greenhouse or cold frame. Those growing in the ground will be fine as long as you cover them with a thick mulch of garden compost or bark chippings.

Grown from rhizomes, canna lilies are essential sun-loving plants for tropical colour. I love the big and brash ones, such as heavily variegated 'Striata' (syn. 'Pretoria'), tall, dark and handsome *Canna indica* 'Purpurea' and the biggest of them all, 'Musifolia', which can grow to a whopping 8 ft. (2.4 m). However, unless you have some pretty big plantless holes in the bed, you should seek out varieties that are slightly more modest in stature. Surprisingly there are quite a few cannas that only reach about 19 in. (48 cm) and make ideal plants for growing in pots. Among them are short and stout 'Délibáb', which has coral pink flowers, bright red 'Gnom' and 'Pallag Szépe', whose flashy flowers are orange with yellow edges.

Although cannas are tender, they are very easy to keep going from one year to the next. If you live in a sheltered area and grow them in the ground, cover them with a thick mulch of bark. In colder areas, cut back the leaves and lift the bulbs with a fork. Clean off the excess soil, and put them in trays of compost somewhere cool and dark before planting out in spring. If you are growing them in pots, wait until the leaves start to yellow in autumn, then cut back the foliage and spent flower stalk to about 1^1/$_4$ in. (3 cm) and move the pots to a shed or greenhouse. Keep the compost damp and bring them out again in May.

Having somewhere to store pots over winter is essential. The year we moved into our house in East London we were without a greenhouse, and I was unwilling to allow my recently assembled collection of cannas (along with other tender bulbs) to take their chances with the elements. For about five months we shared our kitchen with about twenty-five containers pushed up against a wall. Keeping them moist was messy, and my partner, as you can imagine, was none too thrilled.

Dahlias are Cinderella flowers. For many years they were considered passé, a bulb that nobody wanted to grow other than the old boys down at the allotment who were raising them to enter in amateur competitions at flower shows. How things have changed. 'Chic', 'fashionable' and 'desirable' are now the epithets that accompany every mention of dahlias, and many gardeners gush uncontrollably about them, especially if the variety happens to have dark flowers or foliage.

So can you find examples of this trendy tuberous perennial garnishing my patch? Sadly not. I've run out of sunny spaces where I could plant a dahlia, but I can thoroughly recommend the last variety I did grow. It was *Dahlia* 'Pink Giraffe', a double orchid type that made a 40 in. (100 cm) bush, smothered with pink and white flowers. Why do I like it? I think it's one of those rare plants that amuses and impresses me in equal measure. In personality, it's a cross between a clown and a show-girl—the pink and white colour scheme is undoubtedly ludicrous, but with plenty of ooh la la at the same time.

Temporary displays with seasonal plants

If I had to put any group of plants into an imaginary Room 101 (the place in George Orwell's *1984* where you will come face to face with your worst nightmare), it would have to be tender annuals, otherwise known as bedding plants. It's not that I dislike all the plants in this massive tribe—I simply couldn't, as there are some very useful and stunning ones. What I dislike is the way in which they are sometimes used. Beds planted with serried rows of colour or borders edged with marigolds or alyssums are just horrible. Simple as that.

As I have tried to attest, it's not the plants that are at fault, and I grow groups of tender annuals in the garden in summer. They are as cheap as chips and perfect for creating a temporary display that can be used to disguise something unsightly in the garden.

For instance, drains around the outside of the house are not a particularly attractive feature, so I might encircle the edge with some multi-coloured, bushy coleus (*Solenostemon*) grown in pots or possibly some showy New Guinea impatiens. Large containers with an expanse of visible compost are given the same treatment—I space a few small pots of annuals around the edge. This is a clever way of making the most of your space, as you might be able to squeeze five or six plants on the surface of a 30 cm pot planted with a tree.

Spider plants have been mixed with a similar shade of coleus to hide the bare stem of a fig growing in a large pot.

Another trick with annuals is to create a display, mixing them with perennials, grasses and just about anything else that takes your fancy. I do exactly this to add a bit of pizzazz to a redundant gap between my water butt (water barrel) and the wall of a bay window down my side passage. The display is never static, changing during the year either as the mood takes me or when the plants fade and new season annuals become available. A typical summer show might involve Lobelia ×speciosa 'Fan Scharlach' raised up on a large pot as a centrepiece at the back, with spreading clumps of Begonia rex on either side. Carex buchananii raised up on a pot between the begonia and lobelia offers some wispy texture, while taller marigolds or ageratums supply bursts of colour. A perennial Lobelia richardsonii, its pot hidden under a begonia leaf, will have its stems clothed in blue flowers fanned out at the front. Any remaining gaps or ugly pots can be hidden by coleus, spider plants (Chlorophytum) or trailing nasturtium.

Opposite: A temporary display in my side passage masks an ugly plastic water butt (water barrel).

6
Colour Code

UNLESS YOU ARE a complete plantaholic, with an addiction for anything with chlorophyll in its cells and no self-control when confronted by a ravishing specimen you don't already have, it is best to show some restraint when choosing plants for a tiny garden.

Too many plants with different-coloured flowers or foliage can have a chaotic effect when brought together, jarring awkwardly and inflicting grievous harm on the eye (although, of course, there's no accounting for taste, and some owners of gardens planted up like this think the spectacle they have created is beautiful).

A spectrum of colours all elbowed into a minute space can also make a garden appear smaller than it actually is, something that most of us want to avoid. When you are strapped for room, every bit of space becomes extremely valuable. As it is impossible to physically expand a garden beyond confined boundaries, other than to extend the space vertically or by excavating downwards, the aim should be to visually magnify any given extent by using a limited palette of colours to trick the eye into thinking your small garden is larger than it really is.

The plants you pick for your garden go beyond aesthetics. Colours can affect your mood or the atmosphere of the garden. They can also warm the space up or cool it down. For instance, on a hot summer day it can feel extremely repressive to be in a garden that faces due south. On a humid day, without a breeze, you soon start to fry and have to retreat indoors. However, a canopy of plants will give plenty of shade from the sun's scorching rays, and a green colour scheme will provide a psychological cooling effect.

Opposite: A sea of yellow dotted with pink, this meadow may look like it's in the countryside, but it's actually in the heart of Sheffield, Yorkshire. Photograph by Jane Sebire, courtesy of The Garden Collection

159

This colourful small garden has a limited colour range, focussing largely on purples and blues.

If you want to use fiery reds, yellows, oranges or any other bright colours, that is fine, but within a tiny garden it is best to focus on a handful of shades. This could be an incredibly simple scheme, with purple and yellow flowers (which look great together) planted to make an impact against green or bronze foliage plants, or it could be more sophisticated—a small garden I once visited was packed with leafy exotics, but the owners injected accents of colour with orange dahlias, purple sage, dark blue agapanthus and magenta lilies. Since accent plants were used frugally, the display was not overbearing, and the colours worked well together, helping to draw everything together and unify the planting scheme.

When it comes to colour in my own garden, I'm fairly unadventurous. The fences have been painted a gorgeous recessive mossy green, and lovely green in its very many hues is the dominant colour elsewhere, which I make no apologies for. Whether it's ferny, grey or olive green, acid lime, chartreuse, emerald, jade or a zesty spring shade, I simply can't get enough green, and have mixed together so many plants to form a verdant tapestry that gives my space a cool, fresh and lush feel (in fact, and at a complete tangent from gardening, my love of green even goes as far as cars—if I ever get the opportunity, I would love to own a 1968 Jaguar E-type MK. $1^1/2$ in British racing green).

I find it incredibly soothing to look out from my office window on this bosky spot, where hostas knit together with *Pulmonaria*, hellebores, ferns and *Dicentra* within the sleeper bed, or where leafy bamboos on the opposite side of the garden make a towering foil for *Olearia* ×*scilloniensis*, clumps of *Nicotiana*, glossy-leaved *Pittosporum tobira* 'Nanum', box clipped into balls, the divided leaves of *Geranium palmatum* and the green-yellow flowers of several types of *Eucomis*. I've even planted four brown ceramic pots with three plants of *Soleirolia soleirolii* (mind-your-own-business) in different shades of green, which have been placed in an ascending line on top of the sleepers that form the boundary of a bed.

Of course, looking out on the garden is no substitute to actually being outside. When I walk into this green scene after a frantic day in the city or a particularly heavy session pounding the keyboard to meet a tight deadline, I feel instantly at ease. I may have used the term 'urban oasis' a few times during my writing career, but probably none more accurately than to describe the therapeutic effect that my own garden has on me.

Despite its countenance of green, my garden is not bereft of colour. Many of the green foliage plants have flowers, but I've restricted the range of colours to mainly pinks and whites, with a few yellows, which all intermingle well.

Among the pinks are *Thalictrum delavayi* 'Hewitt's Double', an imposing meadow rue that grows well above head height with a flare of wiry stems carrying tiny mauve pompoms. In my sleeper bed is *Sanguisorba officinalis* 'Pink Tanna'—I love many of the burnets, such as fluffy, electric pink *S. obtusa* and shaggy white *S.* 'John Coke', but they need more room than I can provide. Clump-forming 'Pink Tanna' has a mass of stems that grow above knee height and are topped with stumpy pink bottlebrushes. Next to this is the similar-looking but even more diminutive *S.* 'Tanna'. *Dicentra spectabilis* (bleeding heart) is an exceptional transitional plant from spring to summer. It grows in semi-shade and makes mounds of ferny foliage that lie beneath arching stems carrying neatly arranged, pendulous, heart-shaped, pink flowers. Another that grows in shade is *Begonia grandis* subsp. *evansiana*. This hardy begonia makes a handsome clump of shimmering, rounded leaves, then in late summer issues forth sprays that bow under the weight of simple, shell pink flowers. This unusual plant readily forms bulbils in its leaf axils in early autumn that drop to the floor and take root easily. Grasses are also a useful way of providing colour, and I'm head over heels about *Pennisetum orientale* 'Karley Rose', an exceptional grass that makes dense clumps and has slender shoots that bear fluffy pink flowers in summer.

Right: Zingy acid green flowers of *Euphorbia characias* subsp. *wulfenii*.

Below: Three different colours of mind-your-own-business (*Soleirolia soleirolii*) have been planted in pots and placed at different heights on a sleeper wall.

Opposite: Large, leafy plants provide a lush, verdant feel to this tiny garden. Photograph by Nicola Stocken Tomkins, courtesy of The Garden Collection.

In early spring the trellis at the bottom of my garden is a curtain of white.

Whites are represented in my garden by *Valeriana officinalis*, a UK native that is loved by wildlife. It's an imposing plant that has towering, branching stems up to 6 ft. (1.8 m) with tufts of white flowers at the tips. It has a fairly airy form and is probably the closest plant we have to a white version of *Verbena bonariensis*. However, unlike that garden stalwart, the valeriana has a tendency to lean and needs staking to keep upright. *Pittosporum tobira* 'Nanum' is a handsome evergreen shrub with whorls of deep green leaves. Growing to only a fraction of the size of the equally excellent species, it's ideal in a small space, with clusters of creamy white, orange-blossom-scented flowers at the end of the shoots. *Olearia ×scilloniensis* is an evergreen shrub with small, wavy-edged leaves. The foliage is fairly attractive but is completely lost under a blanket of tiny white daisies in summer. My only gripe about this plant is that it is a bit messy—the fluffy seed heads that appear after flowering are not self-cleaning and are not even easily dislodged by the elements. Unfortunately, the overall effect is not particularly attractive, but I'm willing to forgive this plant because of the weeks of super colour it provides. For its long season of flowering, you can't beat *Erigeron karvinskianus*. This spreading daisy thrives on sun and neglect, and I rarely have to water it. It's been planted in several parts of my garden. The white-and-pink-blushed daisies first appear in spring and carry on into late autumn. Sometimes I

A ribbon of white cyclamen for temporary colour.

Geranium palmatum flowers against a backdrop of white olearia.

introduce temporary colour into the garden, and I have great success with *Cyclamen persicum* 'Laser White', a seasonal plant for late-season interest that is bedded out in several places. In my sleeper bed I have planted a ribbon of these among ferns and hostas. The pure white flowers really light up this patch, until the plants turn to mush in late autumn when caught out by frost.

Shades of yellow can be found in the knee-high flower spikes of *Kniphofia* 'Little Maid'. This demure variety of red-hot poker, which is far removed from the typical bright yellow and red clubs that are more symbolic of the common name, has creamy yellow flowers that emerge through a shock of grassy leaves. *Foeniculum vulgare* 'Purpureum' is a handsome fennel with lofty shoots covered in feathery foliage and topped by gorgeous umbels of tiny yellow flowers—these are wonderfully offset by the bronze foliage. Gingers posses the wow factor in great abundance and are essential for a dash of late-summer colour and scent. I was given a large container housing a lemon yellow variety, and the exotic flowers are produced in stout cylinders on the ends of succulent, leafy shoots.

Although I regulate colour in my own garden, I would hate to dictate to anyone else what they should do, as I believe gardening is a great leveller and one thing that we can all be equal in. In theory, creating a garden is all about personal expression, and I think that you should make a garden that pleases you. If that means

Short spikes of yellow emerge from grassy clumps of *Kniphofia* 'Little Maid'.

Yellow flowers of fennel stand out against purple *Cercis canadensis* 'Forest Pansy'.

Need to brighten up your garden in late summer? Try a spicily scented ginger.

breaking all the rules by filling it with a carnival of clashing colours, then so be it. The kind of effect created by marrying together orange roses, white daturas, pink hollyhocks, birds of paradise, yellow marigolds, white dahlias, red-hot pokers and pink fuchsias is not for me, but who am I to find fault if the owner gets a kick out of such a crazy show?

Great combinations

Some gardeners are blessed with a natural talent for placing plants together. Every new perennial they bring into the garden is bought for the sole reason that they know exactly where it should be planted, and their foresight is authenticated when it flowers, creating a happy marriage with whatever plants it has for neighbours.

However, other gardeners are not born with this talent and must follow a more haphazard approach. Sometimes a pleasing plant partnership is accidental—a plant that you couldn't resist buying is brought home and plonked into the only gap left in the garden. The odds are against a fait accompli like this working, but it might if you're lucky.

Great plant combinations are not always the work of the gardener. Many plants self-seed with abandon, and seedlings will pop up wherever they get a sniff of bare soil. The unplanned and unexpected results are often delightful, so resist the temptation to remove every perennial, grass or annual seedling you spot when you're weeding. If in the end the partnership is appalling rather than dazzling, simply evict the squatter with an unceremonious tug.

In my own garden there are plant combinations that have been created by all three of these methods. I am delighted when plants self-seed, as they often plug a hole. The progeny can also be given away to neighbours or provided to folks holding plant sales for charity (message to cynics: yes, I actually do this on a regular basis). It's true that I often search nurseries or the Web for plants that I think will work well with those I already grow, but I'm honest enough to admit that most of the best plant partnerships in my garden are happy accidents.

To my mind, it really doesn't matter how your plant combinations have come together, as long as you are pleased with the results. There's a lot of snootiness in gardening, much of it based around principles put in place by the doyens of my profession, which I think makes painting pictures with plants very intimidating for the average gardener. Don't worry about making mistakes, and don't worry if some eminent gardener has said that certain plants look ghastly together—if you want to try something, go ahead. In the words of one of my favourite authors, William S Burroughs, 'The most dangerous thing to do is stand still'. So trust your instincts, put some plants together and you may create some dynamic duos. The important thing is to do something.

Partnerships could be between two flowers with colours that blend together harmoniously or whose tones contrast (or clash if you're feeling brave), or it could be that one flower shape makes a pleasing foil for another—for instance, the curvaceous blooms of a hellebore teamed with something lighter, such as the dainty, starry flowers of a scilla. Equally, the foliage of a plant might make the perfect backdrop for another plant's blooms, or you might mix different foliage shapes, sizes, colours and textures to create a cool, lush look.

A plant that works well with so many others is *Ophiopogon planiscapus* 'Nigrescens', or black lily turf. This grass-like, clump-forming plant spreads happily near the edge of my sleeper bed and looks well next to my slate shingle path, the bluish hues of the aggregate emphasizing the dark qualities of the plant. In the bed it is conspicuous against the acid green foliage of *Heuchera* Key Lime Pie and makes a suitable backdrop for the white and pink daisies of *Erigeron karvinskianus*, which stand out against the dramatic foliage in stark relief. For a textural effect I have planted *Carex buchananii*, whose slender leaves act as a foil for the wider leaves of the black lily turf.

The black grassy leaves of *Ophiopogon planiscapus* 'Nigrescens' stand out against *Heuchera* Key Lime Pie.

7

How to Keep the Small Garden Going

WHILE SOME OWNERS of small gardens lament the lack of elbow room between their boundaries, they should consider themselves lucky when it comes to keeping their gardens going. Tiny plots need far less upkeep than their larger cousins, which means gardeners can spend more time enjoying the space they have created, rather than continually tweaking it into shape. Low-maintenance does not mean no-maintenance, however—even the most minuscule patch needs some care to ensure it remains looking fabulous.

Composting

Ask someone with a large garden whether it's worth considering a compost bin if your garden is tiny, and they are likely to say no. They have a point. Look through the catalogues sent out by horticultural sundry companies and you'll find lots of great bins that are perfect for turning waste into crumbly, rich compost, but as they frequently measure 39 in. high by 31 in. wide, there is a danger that they will soon become the main focal point of the garden. Well, feel free to question my green credentials, but I don't want my patch dominated by a bin that looks like a black plastic Dalek from *Doctor Who*, even if it does have an impressive 330-litre storage capacity that will easily 'ex-ter-mi-nate' all the garden waste I can generate.

    I talk from experience. When I moved into my current house, the first thing I did, even before I knocked down a dilapidated shed, got rid of the weedy turf and

Opposite: To get the most out of a greenhouse, ensure that it has plenty of storage. I built two three-tiered staging units on either side of the door. Photograph by Caroline Hughes.

173

wrenched some overgrown, disease-ridden shrubs from the ground, was go out and buy a compost bin from the Environment and Regeneration unit of my local council. I'd long wanted to do my bit for the environment, so I felt it was my duty to become a home composter, and the fact that the bin was only £12 (about $18, a subsidized rate offered by the local authority) was the icing on the cake.

I felt as proud as punch when I placed the bin in my new garden, and it didn't take long to fill. I was on a mission to eject everything and leave myself with a blank canvas, so the shreddings from a huge rhododendron, lilacs, forsythia and other shrubs were soon bulging out the top. The problem came when I had finally removed everything from the garden. Now I was ready to lay down the structure for my dream garden, but there was one thing getting in the way—yes, the black compost bin. I didn't want to design my garden around it, so there was nothing for it. I overturned the bin, put all the chippings into bags and took them down to the local rubbish dump where they were consigned to the green waste bay. Fortunately there is a happy ending to this tale. The Dalek lives on, but in my parents' rather more expansive rural garden.

So is it possible to make compost in a tiny garden, without having your space dominated by a bin? Yes. All you need to do is buy a compact wormery. I have a four-tier bin that keeps a low profile in a corner outside my kitchen door. It might be only 29 in. high by 19 in. wide, but it has an army of worms inside that happily

After a few months, kitchen waste turns into lovely, rich, dark compost.

chomp their way through most of my kitchen waste to leave behind brilliant, dark brown compost.

It's a fabulous system. To set it up, fill the first tray with some damp coir and then add worms—my kit came with a thousand red and dendra worms. Vegetable peelings, tea bags, banana skins, coffee grounds, waste bread, egg shells, the odd flower-head and bits of newspaper can then be sprinkled on top (to ensure speedy composting, shred or cut everything up into small pieces). When the worms have eaten their way through a full tray of waste, they will migrate to the next tray up, which can then be filled with waste as before. Apart from the compost, there is a sump at the bottom that collects liquid from the rotting vegetable matter, which is delightfully known as worm tea due to its brown colour. This can be accessed by a tap and diluted with water to be used as an organic plant food.

Composting leaves

Falling autumn leaves can become a bit of a pain, especially as they still seem to find their way into my garden well into February. Where on earth have they come from at that time of year? I've absolutely no idea, but as most of the trees in my area are completely bare by about the middle of November, I suspect they have been released by a neighbour as a practical joke.

Whatever their origin, there's no doubt that they are a nuisance. They blow up against my front door, collect in drains and choke up my flower beds and borders. But rather than pulling my hair out in irritation and consigning all the leaves to the wheelie bin with a few deft strokes of the broom, I turn them into a compost known as leaf mould.

It may not have an appetizing name, but leaf mould is a fabulous material. It can be used as a conditioner to boost the fertility and water-retaining ability of soil, or as a mulch around plants. Hornbeam, oak, beech, sycamore, horse chestnut and the leaves from many other deciduous trees are ideal. Those shed by evergreen trees are best fed through a shredder first as they can take up to three years to rot down.

If you have a large garden it's easy to make this material by erecting a simple square bay with four tree stakes and a roll of chicken wire. All you need to do is secure the wire to the fence with galvanized U-staples. However, those of us with a tiny patch don't have space for a leaf bin, so we need to think small.

An easy way to make leaf mould is to store leaves in black plastic bin liners. To do this, puncture several holes in the base and sides of the bag, which will help drainage and allow air to flow through the bag, preventing leaves from turning slimy. Rake up leaves regularly and stash them in the bag. When it is almost full, ensure the leaves are damp by sprinkling with water, then shake and tie up the bag. Lots of plastic bags will look ugly lying around the garden, so store them out of the way—a shady spot behind a shed is ideal. A more attractive alternative to a bin liner is a jute sack. These are loosely woven to allow in air, but will store leaves in exactly the same way.

When you open the bags next autumn, you'll find the leaves have changed into a crumbly material that makes an ideal mulch. Leave it another year and it will rot down further to make a dark brown compost, which can be dug into the ground as a soil conditioner. This material contains high levels of humus, which helps soil to retain moisture and nutrients.

Saving water

During the summer of 2006 I was taught a valuable lesson: don't take water for granted. Like fourteen million other people across the south-east of England, I was banned from using a hosepipe after the region suffered its driest fifteen months in more than seventy years. Many gardeners moaned about how gruelling it would be trying to keep their gardens alive using a watering can alone, and those with large gardens certainly had their fitness put to the test. However, for me it was a chore, not a hardship. It meant spending an hour in the morning, and a similar amount of time in the evening, walking backwards and forwards from the house to fill up watering cans. Most of my plants made it through the hosepipe ban, although some did turn up their toes and go up to the great plant heaven in the sky.

Despite the fact that I still had access to water, it got me thinking. What would happen if the water levels in our reservoirs and underground aquifers became dangerously low again? Would we be banned from watering our gardens with mains water altogether? It was a possibility, so I decided to give myself an insurance policy—I installed a water butt (water barrel).

Ideally I'd like an underground rain water harvesting system or a large-capacity butt that holds 185 gallons (700 litres) of rain water, but the expense and upheaval of the harvesting system is prohibitive, and a giant water butt would stand out like, well, a giant butt. The answer was the aptly named Space Saver Water Butt, a slimline model that hugs the wall but still has enough room to store 25 gallons (100 litres) of water. Measuring only 37 in. (94 cm) tall by 15 in. (38 cm) wide, it fits brilliantly against the side wall of my house and collects the rain water from the gutter over a bay window porch.

While butts are easily attached to the downpipes of a house, you could also consider fixing one to a greenhouse, shed, outdoor office or any other garden building with gutters and a downpipe. If the building doesn't have gutters, grab your toolkit—it shouldn't be a huge task for someone with moderate DIY skills to install the necessary pipework.

If you really want to be water-wise, you could install an automatic irrigation system to your butt. To keep borders damp, consider attaching a soaker hose to the system, or use micro-tubing with nozzle attachments to water plants growing in containers. Make sure to place a submersible pump into the butt to ensure there is enough pressure to drive the water out.

Common sense dictates that the contents of my water butt will never replace the use of mains water in my garden, but it does give me something to fall back on if there's ever another ban, and it's essential for watering some of my fussier specimens, such as blueberries and carnivorous plants. Apart from the practical side, it also gives me a nice rosy glow, easing my conscience slightly to know that I'm not squandering this valuable resource.

A slimline water butt (water barrel) is easy to fit and takes up very little room.

Pot care in summer

Do you spend your summer holidays fretting about how your plants in containers are doing back at home? If so, take heart—you're not alone. I even know one respected garden writer who won't take a break at all because she's so afraid that her treasures are going to shrivel up and die in her absence. Well, I may love my garden, but I'm darned if it's going to dictate whether I can kick back and enjoy a summer sojourn. Besides, there are plenty of things you can do to keep your plants healthy while you're away, leaving you ample guilt-free time to splash around in the pool or sip a glass or two of ice-cold beer.

The obvious way to ensure that your plants don't get thirsty is to sweet-talk a neighbour into popping into your garden a couple of times a day. I find that bribing generally works—you could offer to look after their cat for a weekend or bring them back some of the local fire-water. Of course, having a neighbour visit guarantees your plants will remain damp, but it comes with a warning. Be prepared for those dreaded words, "I'm sorry, but one of your plants isn't doing that well." This will almost certainly be a prized rarity that you've had for more than twenty years and treated like part of the family. Don't lose your temper, panic or burst into tears. Simply smile and say that you're sure it will be okay.

If you don't have a green-fingered neighbour, or you simply don't trust them, then you'll have to use other techniques. As my garden is south facing, plants soon fry if left on my sunny patio or deck, so if I'm going away for a week or longer (in my dreams, never in reality), I cram the dark passage way down the side of my house with plants. This space gets very little in the way of sunshine, so the plants don't dry out as quickly and are under a lot less stress. Before leaving I give them a really good soak—if you have a piece of green shade netting, drape this over them as well to further reduce evaporating. If you don't have a side return, a space under a tree or behind a shed will do. Alternatively, put pots among other plants in your beds or borders, screwing the pots down so they make really good contact with the soil. This will allow them to take up whatever moisture is available. If you only have a few containers, you could even plunge them into the ground by digging a hole and sinking them up to their necks. This would keep them much cooler and allow them to easily draw up moisture from the soil like a wick.

Keeping plants alive in the greenhouse is tricky. The white paint that I daub over the glass in the spring prevents the sun from burning foliage, but temperatures can still build up dramatically inside. To keep things cool, I leave the vents, window and door open, and thoroughly water everything an hour or so before I depart. This includes splashing water all over the staging and floor. Something that I've found really works well for seedlings or small pots is to buy a sheet of capillary matting and spread it in a seed tray. Soak it well and stand the plants on top, allowing them to take up the water when they need it. If you don't fancy the DIY method, buy a self-watering tray kit, which can sit on top of your greenhouse staging. This consists of an aluminium tray that holds a black plastic reservoir covered with capillary matting. It should help to keep plants topped up with water for about two weeks.

It is possible to reduce the need for ever-so-frequent watering by mixing water-retaining crystals into your compost before planting up containers. I always do this with hanging baskets, as I tend to forget to water them. (I've really no idea why I forget them. I must have walked past the one that perished outside my front door at least twice a day.)

Many gardeners mulch the tops of pots with pebbles, grit and other materials to prevent the compost from drying out too quickly. However, I find this only helps to keep compost damp for a few extra days, so don't think you won't have to water for several weeks. In some ways mulching can be a nuisance, as you can't see how dry the compost is, and it's a pain to have to remove the grit to stick your finger in to determine the dampness. However, it does make pots look more attractive and will prevent weeds from germinating.

If I had an outside tap I would definitely set up an automatic irrigation system. These are less complicated versions of those used by professional nurserymen to keep thousands of plants alive, and are extremely easy to put together—if you are any good at building a Lego model, you will have no problem at all.

There are many irrigation systems available in garden centres and DIY stores, with some more sophisticated than others, and with a choice of attachments for watering different parts of the garden. Pick a kit for containers, making sure it has a timing device and enough hose to reach the area that needs to be watered.

Once your system has been set up, attach it to a timer (fitted to an outdoor tap) and programme it to come on once or twice a day, depending on the plants you need to water.

Storage tips

A headache for anyone with a tiny garden is where to store all the paraphernalia that you need for maintenance. Bags of compost, string, hand pruners, tools, pots, seed trays, sheets of horticultural fleece (cover cloth) and all sorts of gadgets need to be stowed away in a dry place, while being easily accessible as you work in the garden.

The average 6 ft. by 4 ft. garden shed is out of the question, unless you want your space to be dominated by a utilitarian timber structure. I'd rather use the room

Wall-mounted sheds can be placed in a redundant corner and have plenty of room for tools. Photograph by Alison Reid.

for growing plants or making a surface for relaxing, and can't think of anything worse than gazing out the windows of the house onto an ugly wooden shed (although I'm in the minority, as most of my neighbours have done exactly that).

When we first moved into our house, we did in fact look out the windows onto the shed we had inherited. It was plonked right at the bottom of the garden and was most definitely the focal point, thanks to its weathered coating of Barleywood blue paint. Demolishing it with a sledgehammer was incredibly cathartic, and afterwards the garden seemed much, much bigger.

The only problem with being shedless was what to do with the clutter from the garden. For a few years I commandeered the kitchen. Hand tools were elbowed into a unit beneath the sink, while spades, forks, rakes and larger items were propped up in a corner. With my house on the verge of turning into dirty, old rag-and-bone man Albert Steptoe's backyard (from the British television series about a junk dealer, which ran as *Sanford and Son* in the United States in the 1970s), I decided I ought to find a better solution.

The answer was . . . a shed. But not just any shed. This was a slimline, wall-mounted shed perfect for a redundant corner. It's great. It measures 52 in. high, 100 in. wide and 18 in. deep, so there's not enough room for me to get inside, but there's plenty of space for lots of bits and pieces. I can even fit in long-handled tools, such as rakes, with the kind of manipulation that would have made Harry Houdini proud.

If I hadn't gone for this shed, I would have bought a wall-mounted tool store. At only 24 in. wide by 48 in. high, this would have been ideal for the passage alongside my house.

Although the shed is great for smaller items, it doesn't have enough room for everything, such as bags of compost, barbecue charcoal, sand for the kids' pit, half-used cans of paint and masses of brightly coloured plastic toys.

To give myself somewhere else to consign this garden clutter, I built a storage bench. This cross between seat and storage is made from bricks, with a timber waterproof lid that can be lifted on and off by hand.

A bench can be built anywhere in the garden, but if you have a sunny space, put it where you can sit and catch some rays—mine is next to the patio, but a deck would be perfect. To be useful, it will need to be 39–60 in. in length and around 22 in. wide. Always aim to use whole bricks to keep it sturdy. If you have a tricky corner that needs a seat, you could try customizing your design to make an L-shaped bench.

Choose bricks that closely match the colour of your house, and use reclaimed stock if possible to give the bench a weathered look. Unless you like the natural beauty of plywood and strips of pine, give the lid a paint job. Exterior-grade paint in a mossy green shade works well in my garden and helps to extend the life of the wood.

Although the bench earns its keep with a TARDIS-like interior (yes, sorry—another *Doctor Who* reference), you do need to be fairly strong to lift the top on and off. If I designed it again, I'd make life easier by finding a way of adding hinges to the lid.

If making a storage bench isn't your forte, you could always buy some storage seats. There are some really funky designs available, including a rather swish one made from galvanized steel and fitted with a fibreglass seat. They're not cheap, but they do look seriously gorgeous and are ideal for placing around an outdoor table.

A brick storage seat has been fitted with a lid that I use for displaying succulents.

Alternatively, if you are planning to put a garden together from scratch and want to add built-in seating, why not design it to include integral storage? A garden just across the road from me is tiny and has a U-shaped seating area at the back that clings to the fence. Made from bricks and then rendered (smoothed with mortar), it has been fitted with wooden seats that lift off. In summer these are covered with cushions to provide a relaxing place to chill out.

Overwintering plants

Walk into some small gardens over winter and it's like entering a pharaoh's tomb— rather than plants, all you can see are lots of white vertical columns resembling Egyptian mummies. Well, that's what I think, but I've always found that growers of exotic plants, who bundle their treasures up in sheets of horticultural fleece, seem to take offence at this analogy.

The amount of time and effort that some gardeners spend on protecting their plants from the cold is incredible. I once interviewed a gardener in the north Mid-

My tender geraniums are vulnerable to frost but can be protected with a sheet of horticultural fleece (cover cloth). Photograph by Alison Reid.

lands of England who protects his grove of hardy Japanese banana (*Musa basjoo*) by encircling them all with several rings of chicken wire stacked on top of each other and then filling the void with straw. To reach the top he needs a ladder, and when he finishes several hours later the resulting column is as stout as the trunk of a venerable oak tree.

Fortunately, as the temperatures in my garden rarely dip beneath 2°C (36°F), I don't need to go to such elaborate lengths to protect my plants. In fact I don't even bother to wrap up my banana plants anymore—although the leaves turn brown and raggedy in autumn, they always burst back into growth in spring. All I do to ensure the roots of the plant remain unscathed is to spread a 2 in. mulch of well-rotted manure over the root area, keeping an area close to the trunk free of the organic matter.

However, if a period of bad weather is forecast, I do give my bananas some temporary protection that can be added in minutes and taken off when the danger has passed. The easiest way is to simply bind the stem with horticultural fleece and secure it with garden twine. A plastic bag placed over the top helps protect the crown.

It is also worth giving impromptu protection to tree ferns and some palms. The quickest way to do this is to gather the fronds upwards as best you can and hold them in place with twine to protect the central growing point. Then wrap a sheet of horticultural fleece around the captive branches. However, if you live in a cold area or have an exposed garden, it's best to err on the side of caution and protect your plants in the autumn. The materials can be left in place until all danger of frost is over in spring.

Fleece is perhaps the most useful material for overwintering plants. To protect my tender *Geranium maderense* I lay a sheet of horticultural fleece over the top and hold it in place with bricks placed around the edges. This keeps the plants in perfect condition until all danger of frost has passed. I use fleece jackets (special covers) to protect early-flowering fruit trees from frost. My apricot generally flowers between February and March, so it can be vulnerable to a cold snap. Rather than leave a jacket on it all the time, which will prevent pollinating insects from reaching the blooms, I slip it on if a frost is predicted and remove it when safe. The bottom of the jacket has a cord that can be pulled to tighten it in place. These come in several different sizes, and it's essential to pick a size that will go over your plants easily or you might knock some flowers off and ruin the crop.

Snow is rarely a problem in London, but there's an occasional flurry. A particularly heavy fall can flatten plants and even break branches, so should be shaken off as soon as possible. Several years ago the weight of snow caught on top of my bamboo canes caused them to bow dramatically, almost forming a tunnel that ran down the garden. After enjoying the natural sculpture for a few minutes, I gave the plants a quick joggle and they sprang back to normal. To ensure plenty of light can penetrate the greenhouse, I also brush the snow carefully off the glass.

Although most of my succulents are taken into the greenhouse or placed on windowsills indoors in the autumn, for the last couple of years I've risked leaving my century plant (*Agave americana*) outdoors. It's been absolutely fine and doesn't seem to mind the cold. The biggest threat to this drought-loving plant is winter rain, so I just rig up a frame over the top of it to keep it dry. I use a sheet of plywood supported on bricks, but you could make use of anything, including a sheet of plastic or even an old umbrella. A neighbour of mine is slightly braver and leaves his haworthia out over winter, sheltering it under a piece of clear plastic corrugated board supported on four timber legs.

Individual perennials, such as *Verbena bonariensis*, are protected with a covering of mulch, as are dahlias, eucomis and my hardy begonias. In past years I would have lifted these, but as my soil is fairly well drained, they have been fine left in place. To give them a little bit of protection I mulch over the top.

To keep plants in the greenhouse snug, I insulate the inside with bubble wrapping in November. Pieces are cut to size to make sure they fit well, especially where there are cracks, such as under the air vents and windows. It's a bit of a chore cutting

Drought-loving plants can be shielded from winter rain with a temporary structure.

all the bits to fit, but once you've done it you can reuse the same pieces year after year. After insulating, a small paraffin heater is placed in the centre of the greenhouse. It's fairly expensive to run, but I don't light it all the time, only when a frost is forecast. It can be a problem if you go away over the festive period—there's only enough fuel for about four or five days in the tank, so it might just run out at a critical time. A better solution for the long term would be to get an electrician to install an outdoor socket and use an electric heater.

Watering, feeding, pest and weed control

I've never particularly enjoyed watering. I think this has something to do with my early career in horticulture, when a spot of watering meant irrigating a whole container nursery by hand. It was a mind-numbing task that took several hours each day, and I don't think I've ever recovered from it. Still, maintaining the plants in my garden is quick and easy in comparison, and for most of the year I manage to keep my treasures alive with a watering can. In summer or during long dry periods, I resort to the hosepipe. For accuracy I attach a lance with a spray head to the end of the hose so I can deliver water directly over the root area. This is less wasteful and so much better than the rough-and-ready method I was forced to use at the nursery, when my stingy boss insisted I stick my thumb over the end to create a spray. Just thinking about it makes me wince, especially the memories of watering in winter— my thumb, after a few minutes of coming into contact with ice-cold water, would go numb and remain so for the rest of the day.

A lot of the plants I grow are hungry beasts and require plenty of nutrients to keep them going. My feeding regime really starts in autumn, when I prepare my garden for winter. After weeding, cutting back some perennials and generally tinkering with the beds, I cover the surface of the soil with a snug carpet of well-rotted farmyard manure. It's great stuff. Apart from helping to insulate the roots of tender plants, it has much, much more going for it. It's a moisture-retentive, weed-suppressing mulch that helps to add goodness back to the soil and improve the soil's structure as it rots.

If you live in the country you should find a ready supply of this marvellous soil conditioner at your local stables. You may sometimes be charged for the privilege, but most are happy to let you collect the material for free. After all, you're helping them to clear up their yard. A word of caution: if the material is fresh, you will need to put it in a compost bay to let it rot for a year—fresh compost is highly potent and will scorch plants. City dwellers may find it more difficult to find a farm or stables nearby. Don't worry. You can readily buy bagged farmyard manure in garden centres, though it is fairly expensive.

When applying manure, do not add any more than a 3 in. layer, and keep a ring around the trunk of plants free from the material. If manure touches the stem it can soften up the bark, making the plant more susceptible to diseases. Also, there's no need to apply it every year, only when the mulch has rotted away.

Early in the season I like to give some of my leafy plants a boost by using a fertilizer high in nitrogen that promotes stems and leaf growth. I use a soluble formulation with a ratio of 25-15-15, which I apply every seven days or so from late March to May. It's particularly effective on bananas—I swear I can even see the plant stretching upwards before my eyes.

The only other feed I use regularly is a liquid tomato fertilizer on some fruit and vegetable plants. Being high in potash, it ensures that my apricots, peaches, aubergines, chilli peppers and tomatoes are plump and juicy. I use it weekly from the appearance of flowers until the crop is ready to be picked.

I never use herbicides to control weeds in my garden, as they simply aren't necessary. My plot is tiny, and I spend so much time in it that I can keep on top of any alien invasions by hand-weeding little and often. Several weeds have become the bane of my life. When I first took the garden on, there were some huge clumps of

Spanish bluebell (*Hyacinthoides hispanica*), a less lovely version of the United Kingdom's native bluebell. As these bulbs spread fast and outcompete our own bluebell, I decided I should try to remove them all by digging the bulbs out by hand. Five years later they still pop up. As soon as I spot one I'm down on my hands and knees, evicting it from the ground with a long-handled trowel.

Hairy bittercress (*Cardamine hirsuta*) is another persistent and unwelcome visitor. This rosette-forming plant is a real survivor. Each seedpod packs about twenty seeds, which when ripe are fired up to 1 m in the air when you brush past them. As an average plant can contain about six hundred seeds, hairy bittercress will quickly colonize empty spaces and seems to love growing in the tops of pots. Being shallow rooted, it is easy to pull up, but it's essential to get to it while it is still in flower and not left to set seed.

Equally dogged in its determination to set up camp in my garden is sun spurge (*Euphorbia helioscopia*). Related to the ornamental euphorbias, this scrappy little annual grows to about 6 in. (15 cm) and has stems topped with acid green flowers. Later, fruit capsules develop that contain virtually indestructible seeds—I was shocked to read that scientists have found that these can still be viable after twenty years of lying in uncultivated ground. Still, plants are easy to pull up, but like all other euphorbias they exude a milky sap that can irritate the skin, so weed with care or wear thin gloves.

A weed seedling
of sun spurge
(*Euphorbia helioscopia*).

Although I'm not an organic gardener, I rarely use chemical controls in the garden. Many pests are easy to control by hand, such as red lily beetle, which is a problem from late spring. The adults chew holes in leaves and lay grubs that continue to chomp away at the foliage. Although you can wipe them out by spraying (in the United Kingdom, systemic pesticides containing thiacloprid can be used), I have never bothered. The bright red beetles stand out like a sore thumb, so it is easy to pick them off and dispatch them with the heel of your shoe. You have to pick them off carefully, though, as they seem to sense you have murder in mind, and try to wriggle away or drop from the plant as an evasion tactic.

Aphids can be a real problem. In the last few years they have taken to swooping in on my aeoniums, ×*Fatshedera lizei*, bananas, strawberries, clematis and the new shoots of many other plants. Although I try to rub them off by hand, they spread quickly, so to prevent distorted leaves or a poor crop, I bite the bullet and spray them. Such a reaction may raise the hackles of some organic gardeners, but what am I supposed to do, let my plants curl up their toes? Er, no thanks. It may be okay to take a relaxed attitude to pests if you have a large garden and more plants than you can shake a stick at, but as every plant in my garden has to earn its place, I want them to remain healthy and attractive.

The stems of a lobster claw (*Clianthus puniceus*) stripped clean by snails.

My cercis tree, *Cercis canadensis* 'Forest Pansy', is a magnet for scale insects, and I control these in two ways, although I have to admit that I have yet to get on top of the problem. If I see a large colony of the hard-shelled insects on the branches, I'll rub them off with my fingers, but otherwise I let the birds eat them. After noticing that blue tits often flutter from branch to branch, pecking them off, I sited a feeder attached to a long pole among the branches, and in this way have managed to attract more birds to the tree to do the work for me.

Like many others, my garden is besieged by slugs and especially snails. I find them everywhere: in my greenhouse, in the branches of my vine, on bird feeders, on the fence and tucking into my tomatoes. Although the damage to these plants is minimal, these pests make doilies out of the fleshy clumps of *Colchicum* leaves and have devastated my *Clianthus puniceus* several times, stripping the leaves until I have been left with a skeletal structure. Generally I collect them by hand and have some target practice against a wall, but if a plant has come under heavy attack I have no qualms about spreading a few slug pellets on the soil beneath it. You can guarantee that next morning you'll find a mulch of snail shells waiting to be swept up.

My peach 'Avalon Pride' is reportedly fairly resistant to peach leaf curl but has been absolutely infested with the disease in the past. This is noticeable in spring,

Peach leaf curl has devastated this peach tree, 'Avalon Pride', and all affected leaves will need to be stripped off.

when the leaves become puckered, twisted and blistered, and the verdant foliage is emblazoned with patterns of pink.

Although the effects on my tree were fascinating, and actually quite pretty, the disease can hamper a tree's performance, so I removed all affected leaves (about a third of them) before the pink patches had a chance to turn into white spores.

Unfortunately, this is a difficult disease to eradicate, but a spray of copper fungicide before the leaves fall, and then several times over winter, usually gives the tree a fighting chance.

Encouraging wildlife

My garden may be minute, but that doesn't stop me wanting to attract wildlife into it. I grew up in the countryside and have always been fascinated by bugs, and I want my children to see some of the creatures that I encountered while growing up. Besides, if you can attract the right creatures into your garden, they will help to control some of the less desirable beasts.

Over the last few years there has been a proliferation of bug boxes on the gardening market. Take a look in a wildlife gardening products brochure and you will find bee houses, ladybird (ladybug) houses, lacewing chambers, mason bee nests, butterfly houses and many more. These come in all shapes and sizes, from simple tubes to an open-fronted frame crammed with pieces of garden cane that provide a place for insects to hibernate—in the spring, they will emerge from their slumber with a voracious appetite for aphids and other pests.

So what should you choose? Well, rather than creating an estate of bug boxes in your garden, I would pick one box that provides different-sized nooks and crannies for a variety of insects. Among my favourites are boxes filled with bark, which are ideal for both lacewings and ladybirds, and boxes filled with plant stems, such as buddleja, cow parsley, teasel and elder—lots of creatures will nest in here, including solitary bees. These boxes are much better for the environment as you can fill them with material from your own garden, rather than relying on canes that have to be flown halfway round the world.

Most boxes can be mounted on a tree or shed wall. If you're trying to attract ladybirds or lacewings, put the box in a north-facing position so that the insects are not woken up too early in the spring when there are very few aphids about. Bug boxes are really easy to make, and most can be knocked together in a few hours. All you need to do is make a square frame out of four pieces of wood and fill it with pieces of stem from the garden. If your DIY skills are non-existent or you are pushed

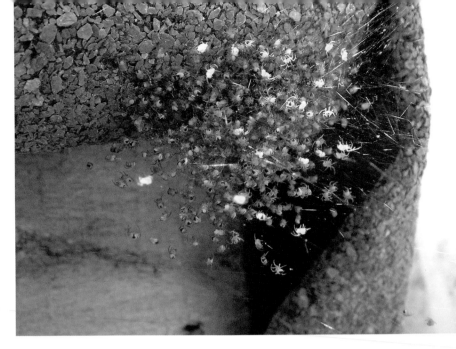

Spiderlings hatch in the outside corner of my shed.

A log wall would make an attractive barrier in a small rural garden, especially when the top has been planted up with small plants. This was seen in a garden in Dumfrieshire, Scotland, and was created to provide a habitat for wildlife.

A bird feeder placed in a border.

for time, there are many ready-made boxes available, which should cost you less than £20 (about $30).

Although a lot of wildlife will hibernate, birds remain active and need a helping hand to get them through the colder months. Ideally you should put out food or hang up feeders in your garden. There are lots of different sorts of feeders available, from clear plastic tube hanging feeders, which are best filled with seeds, to coconut halves filled with fat. Specialist suppliers also have a tasty range of different feeds for different birds, such as black niger seed, which is loved by goldfinches. Rather than make life complicated for myself, I put out a nut feeder for tits, robins and greenfinches and fill a device mounted on a pole with mixed seed that is enjoyed by many wild birds. As long as you don't have cats, you could also sprinkle a few seeds on the floor for ground feeders like blackbirds.

Birds also need to drink and to keep their feathers in good condition, so find space for a birdbath. You do not need anything elaborate—even an old plate will do. Check it regularly and top it up when necessary.

Many of the flowering plants in my garden attract bees, butterflies and hoverflies, but nothing is as popular as the sedum roof on my shed. The nine different sedums put on a floral show from early summer that seems irresistible to these flying

A ladybird (ladybug) larva on a red currant.

A squirrel steals nuts from a bird feeder.

creatures. Even better, the gritty stone base of the roof and the gaps between the plants support many smaller insects and other good guys, like spiders.

Apart from turning your garden into a wildlife sanctuary that literally buzzes with life, many creatures also play an important role in controlling pests. Hedgehogs, birds, beetles and ladybirds all devour nasty bugs, so keep them happy and the more unlikely it is you'll have to resort to chemical controls.

Unfortunately, my garden is also visited by creatures that I don't want: pests such as whitefly, greenfly, blackfly, lily beetles, mealy bug, scale insect and larger creatures such as grey squirrels and urban foxes. I have no qualms about violently dispatching the smaller pests, but I tolerate the cuddlier visitors even though they can wreak damage. The squirrels uproot bulbs, dig around the tops of pots and eat developing fruit—I have to guard my apricot carefully as they can quickly strip it.

Foxes are great fun to watch, especially if they have their cubs in tow, but they stink to high heaven. They leave evil-smelling faeces in the garden and urinate with abandon—avoid getting any on your hands or you'll be rubbing away with the soap and nailbrush like Lady Macbeth for hours. Another problem they cause me is that they seem to like tunnelling under fences, leaving huge holes and ripping up the roots of plants as they go. As they are so adept at scaling fences, I wonder why they bother, although a neighbour claims they are probably digging for worms, a natural part of their diet in the wild. It would seem the urban fox isn't just content to eat abandoned pieces of fried chicken and leftover chips that litter the streets around our local fast food restaurants.

Bed and border chores

In the second week of November, I usually do my final weeding and remove any other debris from the beds. I then give everything a good mulch using well-rotted farmyard manure, spread to about 3 in. deep. I've already extolled the virtues of this material as a soil conditioner, but it also protects tender bulbs and the roots of some of my more vulnerable plants from frost. This includes bananas, grape vine, *Verbena bonariensis* and eucomis. Even though the smell won't clear your nasal passages like the fresh stuff, it's always best to wear gloves when handling it, as it's difficult to get the odour off your hands. Trust me, I've made the mistake.

When you have a small garden, you have to be more ruthless with self-seeded plants than if you were blessed with a big plot. The predominance of a single variety is instantly noticeable, so you have to edit out seedlings with cold-hearted ruthlessness. Still, this isn't easy, especially if you like the plant or if it is fairly rare, and I

Some plants are prolific self-seeders, depositing their progeny in places you would struggle to plant up yourself. But this *Verbena bonariensis* seedling had to go, as it was growing in a crack between paving slabs right in the centre of the path that runs down the side of my house.

often feel a tinge of guilt while pulling a garden gate crasher from a spot where it feels happy to set up camp.

Perhaps the most prolific self-seeder in my garden is *Geranium maderense*. A single plant is capable of siring scores of offspring, and they appear in great profusion: in pots, gaps in the bed and most commonly among cracks in my slate garden path. I leave seedlings if they fill a bare patch or help to soften some hard landscaping, but most have to go. I give some away and pot up a few for myself as insurance policy, since I have lost specimens of this handsome foliage plant over winter before.

Although I tend to scoop any falling leaves I spot in the garden, I've now taken to leaving the litter of foliage that lies around the base of my bamboo. Not because I'm lazy or because they are too fiddly to pick up (although they are), but because I recently read that they contain bamboo-boosting silica. As the leaves rot down, the nutrient is released into the soil, helping with the development of new canes. Now that's a good excuse for leaving the tidying up.

The Plants in My Garden

WHEN I INHERITED my terraced home, only a handful of plants grew in the front and back gardens. Today there are around 250 different plants squeezed into just 600 square feet.

Front garden

Acanthus mollis 'Hollard's Gold'—bear's breeches
Arisarum proboscideum—mouse plant
Asarum splendens—wild ginger
Asplenium scolopendrium—hart's tongue fern
Brunnera macrophylla 'Betty Bowring'
Dicentra spectabilis 'Alba'—bleeding heart
Epimedium ×youngianum 'Niveum'
Hacquetia epipactis
Hosta 'Francee'
Hydrangea anomala subsp. *petiolaris*—climbing hydrangea
Luzula sylvatica 'Aurea'—greater woodrush
Maianthemum racemosum—false Solomon's seal
Milium effusum 'Aureum'—Bowles' golden grass
Polystichum setiferum—soft shield fern
Polystichum setiferum Congestum Group

Hedge

Ligustrum ovalifolium—green privet

Bulbs

Brimeura amethystina 'Alba'
Crocus chrysanthus 'Snow Bunting'
Eranthis cilicica—winter aconite
Erythronium californicum 'White Beauty'—dog's-tooth violet
Narcissus 'February Gold'—daffodil

Opposite: With great skill, contrasting shades of dahlias, cannas and lilies can be grown together in a small garden.

Front Garden (continued)

Hanging baskets and pots

Chlorophytum comosum 'Variegatum'—spider plant

Soleirolia soleirolii—mind-your-own-business

Soleirolia soleirolii 'Aurea'—mind-your-own-business

Soleirolia soleirollii 'Variegata'—mind-your-own-business

Back garden

Side passage

Begonia boliviensis 'Bonfire' (in hanging basket)

Hedera spp., variegated—ivy

Prunus armeniaca Flavorcot—apricot

Prunus persica 'Peregrine'—peach

Rubus fruticosus 'Loch Maree'—blackberry

Vaccinium 'Chandler'—blueberry

Vaccinium macrocarpon 'Red Star'—cranberry

Display near water butt (water barrel)

Begonia rex

Carex buchananii—leatherleaf sedge

Chlorophytum comosum 'Variegatum'—spider plant

Hosta 'Platinum Tiara'

Lobelia richardsonii

Lobelia ×*speciosa* 'Fan Blau'

Pennisetum alopecuroides 'Hameln'

Succulents

cactus, various

Crassula spp.

Faucaria tigrina

Gasteria bicolor var. *liliputana*

Haworthia spp.

Haworthia limifolia

Kalanchoe beharensis 'Fang'

Pachyphytum oviferum

Sempervivum, various—houseleek

Patio area

Actinidia deliciosa 'Jenny'—kiwifruit

Asarum splendens—wild ginger

Astelia chathamica 'Silver Spear'

Athyrium niponicum var. *pictum*—Japanese painted fern

Bergenia 'Bressingham White'—elephant's ears

Clianthus puniceus—lobster claw

Correa 'Marian's Marvel'

Euphorbia mellifera—honey spurge

Ficus carica 'Brunswick'—fig

Fragaria vesca—wild strawberry

Gunnera magellanica

Hosta spp., variegated

Hosta fortunei var. *aureomarginata*

Hosta 'Royal Standard'

Lycopersicon esculentum 'Elegance'—tomato

Lycopersicon esculentum 'Hundreds and Thousands'—tomato

Olea europaea 'Veronique'—olive

Punica granatum—pomegranate

Ribes rubrum 'Rovada'—red currant

Rumex acetosa—common sorrel

Saxifraga 'Cotton Crochet'

Sophora microphylla 'Dragon's Gold'

Note that tomatoes 'Elegance' and 'Hundreds and Thousands' may not be available every-where. 'Arkansas Traveler' makes a good substitute for 'Elegance', and 'Red Grape' for 'Hundreds and Thousands'.

Herb planter

Allium schoenoprasum—chives
Artemisia dracunculus—tarragon
Coriandrum sativum—coriander
Mentha spp.—variegated mint
Origanum spp.—marjoram
Persicaria odorata—Vietnamese coriander
Petroselinum crispum var. *neapolitanum*—Italian parsley
Solanum tuberosum 'Mimi'—potato
Thymus citriodorus—variegated lemon thyme

Growing bag

Capsicum annuum 'Apache'—chilli pepper
Capsicum annuum 'Bellboy'—sweet pepper
Capsicum annuum 'Jalapeno'—chilli pepper

Alpine sink

Arabis blepharophylla 'Spring Charm'
Arenaria balearica
Armeria juniperifolia 'Bevan's Variety'—thrift
Campanula poscharskyana
Chaenorhinum origanifolium
Iris danfordiae
Iris 'Harmony' (Reticulata)
Pratia pedunculata
Pritzelago alpina
Saxifraga 'Findling'
Saxifraga paniculata
Silene schafta (pink)—moss campion
Silene uniflora—sea campion

Raised storage seat

Aeonium castello-paivae
Aeonium ciliatum
Aeonium holochrysum

Aeonium percarneum
Aeonium simsii
Aeonium undulatum
Aeonium 'Zwartkop'
Aloe striatula
Senecio serpens

Grape vine fence panel bed and shade bed

Begonia grandis subsp. *evansiana*
Begonia palmata
Eryngium eburneum
Vitis vinifera 'Schiava Grossa'—Black Hamburgh grape

Right bed

Allium cristophii
Arum italicum subsp. *italicum* 'Marmoratum'
Astelia banksii
Buddleja japonica
Buxus sempervirens—box balls
Corokia ×*virgata* 'Sunsplash'
Erigeron karvinskianus—Mexican fleabane
Eryngium agavifolium
Eryngium pandanifolium
Euphorbia characias subsp. *wulfenii*
×*Fatshedera lizei*
Furcraea spp.
Geranium palmatum
Impatiens omeiana
Ipomoea batatas 'Margarita'
Kniphofia northiae—red-hot poker
Libertia peregrinans 'Gold Leaf'
Muehlenbeckia complexa 'Ward' (male form)
Musa basjoo—hardy Japanese banana
Nicotiana mutabilis
Olearia ×*scilloniensis*
Phyllostachys aurea

Right Bed (continued)

Phyllostachys nigra—black bamboo
Pittosporum tobira 'Nanum'
Pseudopanax lessonii
Rubus idaeus 'Glen Ample'—raspberry
Thalictrum delavayi 'Hewitt's Double'
Valeriana officinalis—valerian

Path

Euonymus fortunei Blondy
Ficus pumila—creeping fig
Hedera spp.—ivy

Sleeper bed

Amicia zygomeris
Astelia fragrans
Cercis canadensis 'Forest Pansy'
Chiastophyllum oppositifolium
Crocosmia spp.—montbretia
Dicentra spectabilis—bleeding heart
Dryopteris filix-mas 'Linearis Polydactyla'
Foeniculum vulgare 'Purpureum'—bronze fennel
Fragaria 'Irresistible'—strawberry
Gypsophila paniculata 'Festival White'—baby's breath
Hedera spp., variegated—ivy
Helleborus foetidus
Heuchera Key Lime Pie
Hosta 'Red October'
Hosta 'Royal Standard'
Kniphofia 'Little Maid'—red-hot poker
Ophiopogon planiscapus 'Nigrescens'—black lily turf
Pennisetum orientale 'Karley Rose'
Persicaria microcephala 'Red Dragon'
Polypodium vulgare

Polystichum tsussimense
Pulmonaria spp.—lungwort
Sanguisorba officinalis 'Pink Tanna'
Sanguisorba 'Tanna'
Thalictrum spp.

Trellis at back

Clematis 'Early Sensation'

Deck area

Agave americana—century plant
Eriobotrya japonica—loquat

Carnivorous planter

Dionaea muscipula—Venus flytrap
Drosera capensis—sundew
Sarracenia purpurea—North American pitcher plant
Sarracenia 'Stevensii'—North American pitcher plant

Waifs and strays (plants in pots)

Aeonium arboreum 'Atropurpureum'
Aeonium arboreum 'Magnificum'
Aeonium balsamiferum
Agave salmiana
Alocasia macrorrhiza
Aloe vera
Arisaema costatum
Begonia sutherlandii
Buddleja tubiflora
Eucomis autumnalis subsp. *autumnalis* 'Peace Candles'—pineapple lily
Eucomis bicolor—pineapple lily
Eucomis 'Cabernet Candles'—pineapple lily
Eucomis comosa—pineapple lily

Eucomis comosa 'Sparkling Burgundy'—
  pineapple lily
Foeniculum vulgare—fennel
Fuchsia 'Gartenmeister Bonstedt'
Hedychium spp.—ginger lily
Hedychium greenei—ginger lily
Ipomoea quamoclit 'Cardinal Climber'—
  morning glory
Jasminum polyanthum
Ledebouria socialis
Pelargonium 'Mrs Pollock'

Plectranthus argentatus
Plectranthus ciliatus 'Drege'
Plectranthus ciliatus 'Easy Gold'
Plectranthus madagascariensis 'Variegated
  Mintleaf'
Plectranthus oertendahlii
Salvia elegans—pineapple sage
Solenostemon, various—coleus
Strelitzia nicolai
Tradescantia zebrina
Verbena bonariensis

Fruit (continued)

United States

Adams County Nursery
26 Nursery Road
P.O. Box 108
Aspers, Pennsylvania 17304
tel: (717) 677-8105
www.acnursery.com

Fast Growing Trees Nursery
4475 Morris Park Drive, Suite J
Charlotte, North Carolina 28227
tel: (888) 504-2001
www.fast-growing-trees.com

Nourse Farms
41 River Road South
Deerfield, Massachusetts 01373
tel: (413) 665-2658
www.noursefarms.com

Southmeadow Fruit Gardens
P.O. Box 211
Baroda, Michigan 49101
tel: (269) 422-2411
www.southmeadowfruitgardens.com

Trees of Antiquity
20 Wellsona Road
Paso Robles, California 93446
tel: (805) 467-9909
www.treesofantiquity.com

Nurseries

United Kingdom

The Beth Chatto Gardens
Elmstead Market
Colchester
Essex CO7 7DB
tel: 01206 822007
www.bethchatto.co.uk

Burncoose Nurseries
Gwennap
Redruth
Cornwall TR16 6BJ
tel: 01209 860316
www.burncoose.co.uk

Clock House Nursery
Forty Hill
Enfield EN2 9EU
tel: 020 8363 1016
www.clockhousenursery.co.uk

County Park Nursery
Essex Gardens
Hornchurch
Essex RM11 3BU
tel: 01708 445205
www.countyparknursery.co.uk
(Southern hemisphere plants.)

Crûg Farm Plants
Griffith's Crossing
Caernarfon
Gwynedd
Wales LL55 1TU
tel: 01248 670232
www.crug-farm.co.uk
(Plants for connoisseurs.)

Fernwood Nursery
Peter's Marland
Torrington
Devon EX38 8QG
tel: 01805 601446
www.fernwood-nursery.co.uk
(*Sempervivum* specialist.)

Glenhirst Cactus Nursery
Station Road
Swineshead
Boston
Lincolnshire PE20 3NX
tel: 01205 820314
www.glenhirstcactiandpalms.co.uk
(Large range of aeoniums.)

Hardy Exotics Nursery
Gilly Lane
Whitecross
Penzance
Cornwall TR20 8BZ
tel: 01736 740660
www.hardyexotics.co.uk

Holly Gate Cactus Nursery
Billingshurst Road
Ashington
West Sussex RH20 3BB
tel: 01903 892 930
www.users.globalnet.co.uk/~tmh

Knoll Gardens
Hampreston
Wimborne Minster
Dorset BH21 7ND
tel: 01202 873931
www.knollgardens.co.uk

Langthorns Plantery
Little Canfield
Dunmow
Essex CM6 1TD
tel: 01371 872611
www.langthorns.com

Norwell Nurseries
Woodhouse Road
Norwell
Newark
Nottinghamshire NG23 6JX
tel: 01636 636337
www.norwellnurseries.co.uk
(Unusual shade plants.)

Pennard Plants
The Walled Gardens
East Pennard
Somerset BA4 6TP
tel: 01749 860039
www.pennardplants.com
(Great range of eucomis.)

South West Carnivorous Plants
Blackwater Nursery
Blackwater Road
Culmstock
Cullompton
Devon EX15 3HG
tel: 01823 681669
www.littleshopofhorrors.co.uk

Spinners Garden and Nursery
School Lane
Boldre
Hampshire SO41 5QE
tel: 01590 673347
www.spinnersgarden.co.uk

Sunnybank Vine Nursery
Journey's End
Ewyas Harold
Herefordshire HR2 0EE
tel: 01981 240256
www.vinenursery.netfirms.com

United States

California Carnivores
2833 Old Gravenstein Highway South
Sebastopol, California 95472
tel: (707) 824-0433
www.californiacarnivores.com

Digging Dog Nursery
P.O. Box 471
Albion, California 95410
tel: (707) 937-1130
www.diggingdog.com

Highland Succulents
1446 Bear Run Road
Gallipolis, Ohio 45631
tel: (740) 256-1428
www.highlandsucculents.com

New England Bamboo Company
5 Granite Street
Rockport, Massachusetts 01966
tel: (978) 546-3581
www.newenglandbamboo.com

Out of Africa
1005 Eckard Road
Centerburg, Ohio 430111

tel: (740) 625-5900
www.out-of-africa-plants.com

Plant Delights Nursery
9241 Sauls Road
Raleigh, North Carolina 27603
tel: (919) 662-0370
www.plantdelights.com

Raintree Nursery
391 Butts Road
Morton, Washington 98356
tel: (360) 496-6400
www.raintreenursery.com

White Flower Farm
P.O. Box 50
Route 63
Litchfield, Connecticut 06759
tel: (800) 503-9624
www.whiteflowerfarm.com

Woodlanders
1128 Colleton Avenue
Aiken, South Carolina 29801
tel: (803) 648-7522
www.woodlanders.net

Bulbous plants
United Kingdom

De Jager
The Old Forge
Chartway Street
East Sutton
Maidstone
Kent ME17 3DW

tel: 01622 840229
www.dejager.co.uk

Hart Canna
27 Guildford Road West
Farnborough
Hampshire GU14 6PS
tel: 01252 514421
www.hartcanna.com

National Dahlia Collection
Winchester Growers
Varfell Farm
Long Rock
Penzance
Cornwall TR20 8AQ
tel: 01736 335853
www.national-dahlia-collection.co.uk

United States

Brent and Becky's Bulbs
7900 Daffodil Lane
Gloucester, Virginia 23061
tel: (804) 693-9436
www.brentandbeckysbulbs.com

Bulbmeister.com
10846 Hodge Lane
Gravette, Arkansas 72736
tel: (479) 787-6579
www.bulbmeister.com

McClure and Zimmerman
P.O. Box 368
Friesland, Wisconsin 53935
tel: (800) 546-4053
www.mzbulb.com

Old House Gardens
536 Third Street
Ann Arbor, Michigan 48103
tel: (734) 995-1486
www.oldhousegardens.com
(Heirloom bulbs.)

Van Bourgondien Bulbs
P.O. Box 2000
Virginia Beach, Virginia 23450
tel: (800) 622-9959
www.dutchbulbs.com

Small gardens to visit
United Kingdom

Don Mapp
47 Maynard Road
Walthamstow
London E17 9JE
www.donsgarden.co.uk

National Gardens Scheme
Hatchlands Park
East Clandon
Guildford
Surrey GU4 7RT
tel: 01483 211535
www.ngs.org.uk

28 Kensington Road
Saint George
Bristol BS5 7NB
www.victorianhousegarden.pwp.blueyonder.
    co.uk

Small Gardens to Visit (continued)

United States

Open Days Program
The Garden Conservancy
P.O. Box 219
Cold Spring, NY 10516
tel: (845) 265-2029
www.gardenconservancy.org/opendays/

Garden supplies

Canada

ELT (Elevated Landscape Technologies)
245 King George Road, Suite 319
Brantford, Ontario
Canada N3R 7N7
tel: (866) 306-7773 or (519) 458-8380
www.eltlivingwalls.com
(Living walls.)

United Kingdom

Enviromat—sedum matting
tel: 01842 828266
www.enviromat.co.uk

Harrod Horticultural
tel: 0845 4025300
www.harrodhorticultural.com
(Space Saver Water Butts [water barrels].)

VertiGarden
tel: 0560 1141477
www.vertigarden.com
(Living walls.)

Vital Earth
Blenheim Road
Airfield Industrial Estate
Ashbourne
Derbyshire DE6 1HA
tel: 01335 300355
www.vitalearth.tv
(Kayak Growbags.)

Wiggly Wigglers
tel: 01981 500391
www.wigglywigglers.co.uk
(Worm bins.)

Useful Web sites

Martyn Cox
www.martyncox.biz

RHS Plant Finder
www.rhs.org.uk/rhsplantfinder/plantfinder.asp

Square Foot Gardening
www.squarefootgardening.com

Woodrow Garden Design (Francesca Murray)
www.woodrowdesign.co.uk

Index

Pages in **boldface** include photographs.

Acacia pravissima, 141
Acaena microphylla 'Kupferteppich', 31
Acanthus mollis 'Hollard's Gold', 70, 197
Achillea ageratum, 97
aconite, winter. See *Eranthis cilicica*
Acorus gramineus, 138
Acorus gramineus 'Ogon', 138
Actinidia deliciosa 'Jenny', 96, 198
Adiantum, 38
Adiantum cuneatum. See *Adiantum raddianum*
Adiantum raddianum, 55
Aeonium, 45, 47, 50, 77, 86, 188
Aeonium arboreum 'Atropurpureum', 200
Aeonium arboreum 'Magnificum', 200
Aeonium arboreum 'Purpureum', 45
Aeonium balsamiferum, 200
Aeonium canariense, 46, 47
Aeonium castello-paivae, 47, **48**, 199
Aeonium ciliatum, 199
Aeonium cuneatum, 45, 46, 47
Aeonium 'Frosty', 47
Aeonium holochrysum, 199

Aeonium lindleyi, 47
Aeonium percarneum, 199
Aeonium sedifolium, 47
Aeonium simsii, 199
Aeonium tabuliforme, 45, 47
Aeonium undulatum, 199
Aeonium undulatum subsp. *pseudotabuliforme*, 47
Aeonium urbicum, 47
Aeonium 'Zwartkop', 45, 87, 199
agapanthus, 160
Agave, 45, 46
Agave americana, 184, 200
Agave salmiana, 200
Ageratum, 157
Allium cristophii, **151**, 199
Allium schoenoprasum, 199
Alocasia macrorrhiza, 200
Aloe, 45
Aloe striatula, 199
Aloe vera, 200
amaranth, red, 103
Amaryllis belladonna, 148
Amicia zygomeris, 200
androsace, 50

apple, 105, 108
   'Cox's Orange Pippin', 108
   'Falstaff', 108
   'James Grieve', 108
   'Winter Gem', 108
apricot, **95**, 96, 105, 110, 184, 186
   Flavorcot, 96, 110, 198
   'Garden Aprigold', 110
   'Tomcot', 96
Arabis blepharophylla 'Spring Charm', 53, 199
Arenaria balearica, 53, 199
Arisaema costatum, **150**, 200
Arisarum proboscideum, 197
Armeria, 38
Armeria juniperifolia 'Bevan's Variety', 53, 199
Artemisia dracunculus, 199
arugula. See rocket
Arum italicum subsp. *italicum* 'Marmoratum', 199
Arundinaria, 127
Arundo donax, **131**, **132**
Asarum splendens, 60, 197, 198
Asplenium scolopendrium, 41, 197
astelia, **136**
Astelia banksii, 199
Astelia chathamica 'Silver Spear', 96, 198
Astelia fragrans, 200
Astilbe, 137
Athyrium niponicum var. *pictum*, 198
aubergine, 102, 118, 119, **120**, 186
   'Violetta Lunga', 117
azalea, **20**

baby's breath. See *Gypsophila paniculata* 'Festival
   White'
bacopa, 40
bamboo, **124–125**, **126**–129, 161, 195
   black. See *Phyllostachys nigra*
   heavenly. See *Nandina domestica*
Bambusa, 127
banana, **124–125**, 186, 188, 194
   hardy. See *Musa basjoo*
   hardy Japanese. See *Musa basjoo*

basil, 41, 103, 114, 118
   Genovese, 113, 117
   purple, 104
   Thai, 116
bay, 135
bear's breeches. See *Acanthus mollis* 'Hollard's
   Gold'
beet 'Bull's Blood', 104
beetroot, 102, 113, 118
beetroot of Chioggia, 117
begonia, 77, 184
Begonia boliviensis 'Bonfire', 71, **72**, 198
Begonia grandis subsp. *evansiana*, 60, **61**, 161, 199
Begonia palmata, 60, **61**, 199
Begonia rex, 63, 157, 198
Begonia sutherlandii, 200
Berberis, 38
Berberis darwinii, 33
Bergenia, 32
Bergenia 'Bressingham White', 198
Bergeranthus glenensis. See *Hereroa glenensis*
Betula nigra, 135
birch. See *Betula nigra*
bittercress, hairy. See *Cardamine hirsuta*
blackberry, 99, 105, 108, 110, 198
   'Loch Maree', 110
black-eyed Susan. See *Thunbergia alata*
Black Hamburgh grape. See *Vitis vinifera*
   'Schiava Grossa'
blackthorn. See *Prunus spinosa*
Blechnum, 38
bleeding heart. See *Dicentra spectabilis*
bloodleaf. See *Iresine herbstii*
bluebell, Spanish. See *Hyacinthoides hispanica*
blueberry, 99, 105, 109–110, 198
bok choy. See pak choi
Borinda scabrida, 127
borlotti bean 'Lamon', 117
bottlebrush. See *Callistemon*
bougainvillea, 78, 79, 140
Bougainvillea ×*buttiana* 'Raspberry Ice', 79
Bougainvillea 'California Gold', 79

Bougainvillea Camarillo Fiesta. See *Bougainvillea* 'Orange Glow'

Bougainvillea 'Easter Parade', 79

Bougainvillea 'Monle'. See *Bougainvillea* 'Orange Glow'

Bougainvillea 'Orange Glow', 79

Bowles' golden grass. See *Milium effusum* 'Aureum'

box, 135, 161, 199

Brimeura amethystina 'Alba', 147, 197

Briza maxima, 11, 57

broccoli, 113

broom, pineapple. See *Cytisus battandieri*

brugmansia, 77

Brunnera macrophylla 'Betty Bowring', 70, 147, 197

Brussels sprouts, 102

Buddleja davidii, 38

Buddleja japonica, 199

Buddleja tubiflora, 200

bulrush, 138

Bupleurum rotundifolium 'Green Gold', 57

burnet. See *Sanguisorba*

burnet, salad, 103

burr, New Zealand. See *Acaena microphylla* 'Kupferteppich'

busy Lizzy (impatiens), 55

Butomus umbellatus, 139

Buxus sempervirens, 199

cabbage, Chinese, 103

cactus, 50, 71, 198

Calibrachoa, **45**

Calla palustris, 137

Callistemon, **140**

Callistemon citrinus 'Splendens', 140

camellia, 139

campanula, 50

Campanula portenschagiana, 38

Campanula poscharskyana, 38, 53, 199

Canna, 16, 150, 154, **197**–198

Canna 'Délibáb', 153

Canna 'Gnom', 153

Canna indica 'Purpurea', 153

Canna 'Musifolia', 153

Canna 'Pallag Szépe', 153

Canna 'Pretoria'. See *Canna* 'Striata'

Canna 'Striata', 153

Capsicum annuum 'Apache', 199

Capsicum annuum 'Bellboy', 199

Capsicum annuum 'Jalapeno', 199

Cardamine hirsuta, 187

Carex buchananii, 71, 157, 169, **170**, 198

Carex elata 'Aurea', 137

carrot, 102, 118

    'Parisier Market', 116

carrot leaf, 103

cattail. See *Typha angustifolia*; *T. minima*

cavelo nero. See kale 'Black Tuscany'

cavolo nero. See kale 'Black Tuscany'

ceanothus, 139

celery, 113

Centaurea cyanus 'Black Ball', 57

century plant. See *Agave americana*

Cercis canadensis 'Forest Pansy', 62, 77, 97, 151, **167**, 170, 189, 200

Cerinthe major 'Purpurascens', 57

Cerinthe minor 'Bouquet Gold', 57

chaenomeles, 139

Chaenorhinum origanifolium, 53, 199

Chamaedorea elegans, 55

chard, 118

cherry, 96, 108

chervil, 113, 116

Chiastophyllum oppositifolium, 200

chicory, 103, 118

    'Rossa di Treviso', 117

chile. See chilli pepper

chilli pepper, 102, 118, 119, 120, 186, 199

    'Pinocchio's Nose', 117

    'Thai Dragon', 116

Chimonobambusa, 127

chives, 38, 42, **82**, 99, 199

Chlorophytum, **70**, 71, 77, 157. See also spider plant
Chlorophytum comosum 'Aureomarginata',71
Chlorophytum comosum 'Golden Glow', 70–71
Chlorophytum comosum 'Variegatum', 70, 198
Chlorophytum comosum 'Vittatum', 70
Chusquea, 127
Clavinodum, 127
clematis, 40, 77, 188
Clematis 'Early Sensation', 200
Clematis 'Rouge Cardinal', 40
Clianthus puniceus, **188,** 189, 198
Colchicum, 148, 189
Colchicum autumnale, 148
Colchicum byzantinum, 148
Colchicum cilicicum, 148
Colchicum speciosum, 148
Colchicum speciosum var. *bornmuelleri*, 148
Colchicum 'Waterlily', 39, 148
coleus, **155**, 157, 201
coriander, 98, 99, 113, 116, 199
    Vietnamese. See *Persicaria odorata*
Coriandrum sativum, 199
corn salad, 104
Corokia ×*virgata* 'Sunsplash', 62, 199
Correa 'Marian's Marvel', 96, 198
Corydalis lutea, 38
courgette, 19, 102, 119, 120
cranberry, 105, 109–110, 198
Crassula, 45, 46, 198
Crataegus monogyna, 33
crinum, 148
Crocosmia, 200
crocus, 74
    autumn, 148, **149**
Crocus chrysanthus 'Snow Bunting', 147, 197
currant, 108
    red, 99, 105, **106**, **193**, 198
    white, 99
cyclamen, 148, **165**
Cyclamen cilicium, 148
Cyclamen cyprium, 148

Cyclamen graecum, 148
Cyclamen hederifolium, 148
Cyclamen persicum 'Laser White', 166
Cyrtomium falcatum, 41
Cytisus battandieri, 141

daffodil, 33, 144, 145, 197
dahlia, 16, 130, 150, 154, 160, 184, **197**–198
    tree. See *Dahlia imperialis*
Dahlia imperialis, 130
Dahlia 'Pink Giraffe', 130, 131, 154
daisy, **35**, 38, 164
Darmera peltata, 137
Dianthus 'Calypso Star', 38
Dicentra, 161
Dicentra spectabilis, 161, 200
Dicentra spectabilis 'Alba', 70, 197
Dichondra argentea 'Silver Falls', 72
Dichondra micrantha 'Emerald Falls', 72
Dierama, 38
Dionaea muscipula, 53, 54, 200
donkey's tail. See *Sedum morganianum*
Dracaena sanderiana, 55
Drosera capensis, 53, 54, 200
Dryopteris filix-mas 'Linearis Polydactyla', 200

echeveria, **51**, 86
Echinacea, 32
eggplant. See aubergine
Eleocharis acicularis, 139
elephant's ears. See *Bergenia* 'Bressingham White'
Elodea canadensis, 139
endive 'En Cornet de Bordeaux', 116
Epimedium ×*youngianum* 'Niveum', 70, 147, 197
Equisetum, 11
Equisetum arvense, 138
Eranthis cilicica, 147, 197
Erigeron karvinskianus, 33, 38, 164, 169, 199
Eriobotrya japonica, 133, 200
Eryngium agavifolium, 199
Eryngium eburneum, 199

Eryngium pandanifolium, 199
Erythronium californicum 'White Beauty', 147, 197
escallonia, 33
Eschscholzia californica 'Apricot Chiffon', 57
Eschscholzia californica 'Golden Tears', 57
Eschscholzia californica 'Golden Values', 57
Eschscholzia californica 'Ivory Castle', 57
Eschscholzia californica 'Red Chief', 57
Eschscholzia californica 'Sun Shades', 57
Eucomis, 150, **152**, 153, 161, 184, 194
Eucomis autumnalis subsp. *autumnalis* 'Peace
    Candles', 200
Eucomis bicolor, 200
Eucomis bicolor 'Alba', 153
Eucomis 'Cabernet Candles', 200
Eucomis comosa, 153, 200
Eucomis comosa 'Sparkling Burgundy', 153, 201
Eucomis vandermerwei 'Octopus', 153
Euonymus fortunei, 81
Euonymus fortunei Blondy, 81, 200
Euonymus fortunei 'Duncanata Variegated
    Vegeta', 81
Euonymus fortunei 'Emerald 'n' Gold', 81
Euonymus fortunei 'Silver Queen', 81
Eupatorium, 32
euphorbia, 187
Euphorbia characias subsp. *wulfenii*, **162**, **171**, 199
Euphorbia helioscopia, **187**
Euphorbia mellifera, 96, 135, **136**, 198

Fargesia murielae 'Bimbo', 127
Fargesia murielae 'Simba', 127
Fargesia robusta, 127
Fargesia scabrida. See *Borinda scabrida*
×*Fatshedera lizei*, 60, 143, 188, 199
Faucaria tigrina, 198
fennel, 113, **167**, 201
    bronze. See *Foeniculum vulgare* 'Purpureum'
    Florence. See *Foeniculum vulgare* var. *azoricum*
    purple, 170
fern, **35**, 41, 147, 161, 166
    fishtail. See *Cyrtomium falcatum*

hart's tongue. See *Asplenium scolopendrium*
Japanese painted. See *Athyrium niponicum*
    var. *pictum*
maidenhair. See *Adiantum raddianum*
soft shield. See *Polystichum setiferum*
tree, 183
Ficus carica 'Brown Turkey', 109
Ficus carica 'Brunswick', 109, 198
Ficus pumila, 55, 80, 81, 200
Ficus pumila 'Variegata', 80–81
fig, 96, 105, **109**, **155**, 198
    creeping. See *Ficus pumila*
fleabane, Mexican. See *Erigeron karvinskianus*
Foeniculum vulgare, 201
Foeniculum vulgare var. *azoricum*, 97, 102
Foeniculum vulgare 'Purpureum', 97, 166, 200
Fragaria 'Irresistible', 200
Fragaria vesca, 198
Fremontodendron 'California Glory', 141
French bean, dwarf, 74, 104
fuchsia, 39, 77
Fuchsia 'Gartenmeister Bonstedt', 201
Fuchsia 'Riccartonii', 33
Furcraea, 46, 199

garlic 'Lautrec Wight', 116
Gasteria, 45
Gasteria bicolor var. *liliputana*, 198
gentian, 38, 50
geranium, 77, **183**
Geranium maderense, 184, 195
Geranium palmatum, 50, 161, **165**, **171**, 199
Geranium subcaulescens, 38
ginger, 166, **167**
    wild. See *Asarum splendens*
gooseberry, 38, 109
    Chinese, 96
    'Invicta', 109
    'Remarka', 109
gourd, 19
grape, 108, 194
Gunnera, **133**, 137

Gunnera magellanica, 135, **136**, 198
Gunnera manicata, 132, 135
Gypsophila paniculata 'Festival White', **170**, 200

Hacquetia epipactis, 147, 197
hair grass. See *Eleocharis acicularis*
hare's tail. See *Lagurus ovatus*
Haworthia, 45, 184, 198
Haworthia attenuata, 45
Haworthia limifolia, 198
hawthorn, common. See *Crataegus monogyna*
heather, **20**, 50
Hedera, 198, 200
Hedychium, 201
Hedychium greenei, 201
hellebore, 161, 169
Helleborus foetidus, 200
Herby Salad Leaf Mixed, 104
Hereroa glenensis, 53
Heuchera Key Lime Pie, **169**, 200
Hibanobambusa, 127
holly, 135
honey bush. See *Melianthus major*
honey spurge. See *Euphorbia mellifera*
honeywort. See *Cerinthe major* 'Purpurascens'
Hordeum jubatum, 11
horsetail. See *Equisetum arvense*
Hosta, 11, 148, 161, 166, 198
Hosta fortunei var. *aureomarginata*, 198
Hosta 'Francee', 197
Hosta 'Platinum Tiara', 198
Hosta 'Red October', 200
Hosta 'Royal Standard', 198, 200
houseleek, 46, 48, **49**, 87, 198. See also
       Sempervivum
Hoya carnosa, 79
hyacinth, **33**
Hyacinthoides hispanica, 187
hydrangea, climbing. See *Hydrangea anomala*
    subsp. *petiolaris*
Hydrangea anomala subsp. *petiolaris*, 197
Hypoestes phyllostachya, 55

impatiens, New Guinea, 155
Impatiens omeiana, 62, 199
Impatiens tinctoria, 129, **130**
Indocalamus, 127
Ipomoea alba, 77
Ipomoea batatas, 72
Ipomoea batatas 'Blackie', 72
Ipomoea batatas 'Margarita', 72, 199
Ipomoea batatas 'Pink Frost', 72
Ipomoea batatas 'Variegata'. See *Ipomoea batatas*
    'Pink Frost'
Ipomoea lobata, 78
Ipomoea purpurea 'Caprice', 78
Ipomoea purpurea 'Grandpa Otts', 78
Ipomoea quamoclit 'Cardinal Climber', 78, 201
Ipomoea tricolor 'Heavenly Blue', 78
Iresine herbstii, 55
iris, **30**–31, 137
Iris danfordiae, 53, 199
Iris 'Harmony' (Reticulata), 53, 199
Iris laevigata, 137
Iris pseudacorus, 137
Iris reticulata, 146
Iris versicolor, 137
Italian Salad Collection, 103–104
ivy. See *Hedera*
    Boston, 40
    English, 80
    Swedish. See *Plectranthus*
    tree. See ×*Fatshedera lizei*
    variegated, 71

Japanese maple, **20**, 135
jasmine, 139
Jasminum polyanthum, 68, 201
Jovibarba, 47–48
Juncus decipiens 'Curly-wurly', 138
Juncus decipiens 'Spiralis Nana', 138
Juncus inflexus 'Afro', 138
juniper, 38, 135

Kalanchoe beharensis 'Fang', 198
kale, black. See kale 'Black Tuscany'
kale 'Black Tuscany', 97, 102
kale 'Red Russian', 103
kawakawa. See *Macropiper excelsum*
kiwifruit. See *Actinidia deliciosa* 'Jenny'
Kniphofia 'Little Maid', **166**, 200
Kniphofia northiae, **149**, 199
komatsuna, 103

Lagarosiphon major, 139
Lagurus ovatus, 57
land cress, variegated, 98
Lantana, 63
Ledebouria socialis, 201
lemon grass, 116
lettuce, 41, 119, 120
    'Freckles', 97
    'Lollo Rossa', 97, 103–104
    'Lollo Rosso', 97, 103–104
    salad bowl, 99, 104
Libertia, 11
Libertia peregrinans 'Gold Leaf', 199
ligustrum, 135
Ligustrum ovalifolium, 197
lilac, 23
Lilium formosanum var. *pricei*, **142–143**, 152
lily, 150, 152, 160, **197**–198
    arum, 137
    canna, 153
    dwarf formosa. See *Lilium formosanum* var.
        pricei
    ginger. See *Hedychium*
    pineapple. See *Eucomis*
lily turf, black. See *Ophiopogon planiscapus*
    'Nigrescens'
Limnanthes douglasii, 57
Linaria, 38
Lobelia richardsonii, 157, 198
Lobelia ×*speciosa* 'Fan Blau', 198
Lobelia ×*speciosa* 'Fan Scharlach', 157
lobster claw. See *Clianthus puniceus*

Lophospermum 'Red Dragon', 68
loquat, 105, 133, 200
love-in-a-mist. See *Nigella*
lungwort. See *Pulmonaria*
Luzula sylvatica 'Aurea', 70, 146–147, 197
Lycopersicon esculentum 'Elegance', 198
Lycopersicon esculentum 'Hundreds and
    Thousands', 198
Lysichiton americanus, 137
Lysimachia minoricensis, 62

mace. See *Achillea ageratum*
Macropiper excelsum, 62
Magnolia grandiflora, 135
Magnolia grandiflora 'Little Gem', 135
Maianthemum racemosum, 70, 147, 197
Maranta leuconeura var. *erythroneura*, 55
marigold, 119, 120, 157
    African, 55
marjoram, 104, 199
Maurandya barclayana, 68
Maurandya 'Bridal Bouquet', 68
Maurandya 'Red Dragon'. See *Lophospermum* 'Red
    Dragon'
meadow foam. See *Limnanthes douglasii*
meadow rue. See *Thalictrum delavayi* 'Hewitt's
    Double'
Melianthus major, **134–135**
Mentha, 199
Mentha requienii, 31
Milium effusum 'Aureum', 147, 197
Mina lobata. See *Ipomoea lobata*
mind-your-own-business. See *Soleirolia soleirolii*
mint, 42, 99
    Corsican. See *Mentha requienii*
    variegated, 199
Miscanthus, 11
Miscanthus sinensis 'Ferner Osten', 32
mixed salad leaves, 98
mizuna, 103, 104
monkey cups. See *Nepenthes*
Monstera deliciosa, 63

montbretia. See *Crocosmia*
moonflower. See *Ipomoea alba*
morning glory. See *Ipomoea*
moss campion. See *Silene schafta*
mouse plant. See *Arisarum proboscideum*
Muehlenbeckia complexa 'Ward' (male form), 199
Musa basjoo, 77, **107**, 183, 199
muscari, 33, 74
mustard, 98
    'Giant Red', 104
    'Golden Frill', 104
    green, 103
    oriental, 116–117
    'Pizzo', 104
    purple, 103
    red, 113
    'Red Frills', 104
    'Ruby Streaks', 104
Myosotis scorpioides, 139
Myriophyllum aquaticum, 139
Myriophyllum verticillatum, 139

Nandina domestica, 135
narcissus, dwarf, 71, 74
Narcissus 'February Gold', 147, 197
Narcissus 'Tête-à-tête', **145**
nasturtium, 40, 104, 119, 120, 157, **171**
nectarine, 96, 105, 110
    'Lord Napier', 110
    'Nectarella', 110
Nepenthes, 71
nerine, 148
Niche Salad Leaves Blend, 103
Nicotiana, 161
Nicotiana mutabilis, 170–171, 199
Nigella, 57
Nigella damascena 'Miss Jekyll', 57
Nigella papillosa 'African Bride', 57
Nigella papillosa 'Midnight', 57
Nymphaea 'Aurora', 139
Nymphaea 'Joanne Pring', 139
Nymphaea tetragona 'Alba', 139

Nymphaea tetragona 'Johann Pring'. See
    Nymphaea 'Joanne Pring'

Olea europaea 'Veronique', 112, 198
olearia, **165**
Olearia ×*haastii*, 38
Olearia ×*scilloniensis*, 161, 164, 199
olive, 105, 110, 198
    'Veronique', 110–**111**
onion, 41
    Japanese bunching, 117
    'Rossa Lunga di Firenze', red salad, 117
    spring, 118
Ophiopogon planiscapus 'Nigrescens', **169**, 200
Origanum, 199
oven's wattle. See *Acacia pravissima*
Oxalis, **73**, 77
Oxalis 'Black Velvet', 73
Oxalis 'Burgundy Wine', 73
Oxalis 'Frosted Jade', 73

Pachyphytum oviferum, 198
pak choi, 103
palm, **124–125**, 183
parlour palm. See *Chamaedorea elegans*
parrot's feather. See *Myriophyllum aquaticum*
parsley, 41, 99
    Italian. See *Petroselinum crispum* var.
      neapolitanum
parsnip, 114
passion flower, **64–65**
pea, 113
    Chinese. See snow pea
    Oregon sugar pod, 113
    snow, 113
peach, 96, 110, 186, 198
    'Avalon Pride', **189**
    'Bonanza', 110
    'Peregrine', 110
pear, 105, 108
    'Concorde', 108
    'Conference', 108

'Terrace Pearl', dwarf, 108–109
Pelargonium 'Mrs Pollock', 201
Pennisetum alopecuroides 'Hameln', 198
Pennisetum orientale 'Karley Rose', 161, 200
Pennisetum thunbergii 'Red Buttons', 32
Persicaria microcephala 'Red Dragon', **170**, 200
Persicaria odorata, 199
Petroselinum crispum var. *neapolitanum*, 199
petunia, 39, 40, 55, 71
Phlomis italica, 97
Phlox stolonifera compact, 38
Phyllostachys, 127
Phyllostachys aurea, 126, 199
Phyllostachys nigra, 50, 62, 126, 127, **128**, 200
pitcher plant, North American. See *Sarracenia purpurea*; *S.* 'Stevensii'
Pittosporum tobira 'Nanum', 161, 164, 200
Plectranthus, 73, **74**
Plectranthus argentatus, 201
Plectranthus australis. See *Plectranthus verticillatus*
Plectranthus ciliatus 'Drege', 201
Plectranthus ciliatus 'Easy Gold', 73, 201
Plectranthus madagascariensis 'Variegated Mintleaf', 73, 201
Plectranthus oertendahlii, 201
Plectranthus verticillatus, 55
Pleioblastus, 127
plum, 108
polka dot plant. See *Hypoestes phyllostachya*
Polypodium, 38
Polypodium vulgare, 200
Polystichum setiferum, 147, 197
Polystichum setiferum Congestum Group, 70, 197
Polystichum tsussimense, 200
pomegranate, 105, **107**, 112, 198
pondweed, Canadian. See *Elodea canadensis*
poppy, California, 57
potato, 102, 199
'Mimi', **102**
Pratia pedunculata, 53, 199
Pratia pedunculata 'County Park', 53

prayer plant. See *Maranta leuconeura* var. *erythroneura*
primrose, **34**
Primula, 11
Primula beesiana, 137–138
Primula pulverulenta, 137–138
Primula vulgaris, **34**
Pritzelago alpina, 53, 199
privet, green. See *Ligustrum ovalifolium*
Protea, 63
Prunus armeniaca Flavorcot, 198
Prunus persica 'Peregrine', 198
Prunus spinosa, 33
Pseudopanax crassifolius, **12 13**
Pseudopanax lessonii, 62, 200
Pseudopanax lessonii 'Gold Splash', 62
Pseudosasa, 127
Pulmonaria, 161, 200
Punica granatum, 198
purslane, golden, 103
pyracantha, 139

quaking grass, 39
quaking grass, big. See *Briza maxima*

radicchio, 104
radish, 41
   Chinese, 116
   'Plum Purple', 116
   purple, 113
radish leaf, 103
raspberry, 96, 108, 200
red-hot poker. See *Kniphofia* 'Little Maid'; *K. northiae*
reed, Spanish. See *Arundo donax*
reed mace, lesser. See *Typha angustifolia*
Rheum palmatum, 137
Rhipsalidopsis, 70
Rhipsalis, 71
rhododendron, 23, 24
Rhodohypoxis baurii, 53
rhubarb, giant. See *Gunnera manicata*

ribbon plant. See *Dracaena sanderiana*
Ribes, 38
Ribes rubrum 'Rovada', 198
rocket, 98, 104, 113, 118
    wild, 117, 119, 120
roquette. See rocket
rose, 23, 33, 77
rosemary, 23, 41, 97
Rosmarinus officinalis Prostratus Group
    'Capri', 97
Rubus fruticosus 'Loch Maree', 198
Rubus idaeus 'All Gold', 96
Rubus idaeus 'Glen Ample', 96, 200
rucola. See rocket
Rudbeckia fulgida var. *deamii*, **171**
Rumex acetosa, 198
runner bean 'Fandango', 119, 120
rush, Japanese. See *Acorus gramineus*

sage, 32, 160
    golden variegated. See *Salvia officinalis*
      'Icterina'
    Jerusalem. See *Phlomis italica*
    pineapple. See *Salvia elegans*
Sagittaria sagittifolia, 139
saladini, oriental, 103
salad leaves, 118
Salvia elegans, 201
Salvia officinalis 'Icterina', 97
Sanguisorba, 11
Sanguisorba 'John Coke', 161
Sanguisorba obtusa, 161
Sanguisorba officinalis 'Pink Tanna', 161, 200
Sanguisorba 'Tanna', 161, 200
sarracenia, 54
Sarracenia purpurea, 53, 200
Sarracenia 'Stevensii', 53, 200
Sasa, 127
Sasaella, 127
saxifrage, 50
Saxifraga 'Cloth of Gold', 53
Saxifraga 'Cotton Crochet', 60, **136**, 198

Saxifraga 'Findling', 53, 199
Saxifraga paniculata, 53, 199
Schizostylis, 150
scilla, 169
Scilla autumnalis, 148
scrambled egg plant. See *Limnanthes douglasii*
sea campion. See *Silene uniflora*
sedge, leatherleaf. See *Carex buchananii*
sedum, 39, 41, 45, **82**, 83, 86, **87**, **171**, 192
    purple, 32
Sedum acre, 41, 87
Sedum album, 41
Sedum 'Autumn Joy', 41
Sedum kamtschaticum, 41
Sedum morganianum, 71
Sedum pulchellum, 41
Sedum reflexum. See *Sedum rupestre*
Sedum rupestre, 41
Sedum sexangulare, 41
Sedum spathulifolium 'Cape Blanco', 53
Sedum spurium, 41
Sedum spurium 'Variegatum', 53
Sedum telephium 'Purple Emperor', 171
Selaginella kraussiana 'Aurea', 55
Semiarundinaria, 127
Sempervivum, 47–48, 49, 50, 53, 198. See also
    houseleek
Sempervivum arachnoideum, 49
Sempervivum 'Atropurpureum', 49
Sempervivum calcareum 'Extra', 49
Sempervivum 'Gallivarda', 48
Sempervivum 'Madeleine', 49
Sempervivum montanum subsp. *montanum*, 49
Sempervivum 'Othello', 49
Senecio serpens, 199
Setcreasea pallida 'Variegata'. See *Tradescantia*
    pallida 'Purpurea'
shallot 'Banana', 116
shallot 'Jermor', 116
silene, 50
Silene maritima. See *Silene uniflora*
Silene schafta, 53, 199

Silene uniflora, 53, 199
Sinobambusa, 127
Sisyrinchium, 11, 32
Sisyrinchium 'Californian Skies', 38
skunk cabbage, North American yellow. See
      Lysichiton americanus
Smilacina racemosa. See *Maianthemum racemosum*
snowdrop, 144, 145, **146**
snow pea, 113
Solanum tuberosum 'Mimi', 199
Soleirolia soleirolii, 161, **162**, 198
Soleirolia soleirolii 'Aurea', 198
Soleirolia soleirollii 'Variegata', 198
Solenostemon, 155, 201. See also coleus
Solomon's seal, false. See *Maianthemum*
      racemosum
Sophora microphylla 'Dragon's Gold', 198
sorrel, common. See *Rumex acetosa*
sorrel, French, 116
spider plant, **70**, 71, 77, **155,** 157, 198
    common variegated. See *Chlorophytum*
      comosum 'Variegatum'
spiderwort. See *Tradescantia*
spinach, oriental, 117
squash, 19, **51**, 102
Sternbergia, 148
Stipa gigantea, 11
strawberry, 38, 105, **106**, 188, 200
   alpine, 74, **99,** 105
   wild. See *Fragaria vesca*
Strelitzia nicolai, 201
sundew. See *Drosera capensis*
sunflower, **18**, 19, 113
sun spurge. See *Euphorbia helioscopia*
sweet pepper, 102, 118, 199
sweet potato. See *Ipomoea batatas*
Swiss chard 'Bright Lights', 97, 113
Swiss chard of Lyon, 116
Swiss cheese plant. See *Monstera deliciosa*

tamarix, 33
tarragon, 42, 199

Thalictrum, 200
Thalictrum delavayi 'Hewitt's Double', 151, 161,
    200
thrift, 199
Thunbergia alata, 39
thyme, **36**–**37**, 41, 97, 102
   variegated lemon. See *Thymus citriodorus*
Thymus citriodorus, 199
Thymus Coccineus Group, 31
Thymus pseudolanuginosus, 31
Thymus serpyllum 'Pink Chintz', 31
tiger flower. See *Tigridia*
Tigridia, 150
tomato, 73–74, 118, 119, 120, 186, 198
   'Arkansas Traveler',198–199
   'Elegance', 198–199
   'Hundreds and Thousands', 74, **75,** 198–199
   'Marmande', 116
   'Red Grape', 74, 199
   'Roma', plum, 117
Trachelospermum asiaticum, 81
Trachelospermum jasminoides, 81
Tradescantia, 71
Tradescantia pallida 'Purpurea', 71
Tradescantia zebrina, 71, 201
Tropaeolum majus 'Alaska', 119, 171
tulip, 150
Typha angustifolia, 137
Typha minima, 138

Vaccinium 'Chandler', 109–110, 198
Vaccinium macrocarpon 'Red Star', 109–110, 198
valerian. See *Valeriana officinalis*
Valeriana officinalis, 164, 200
Venus flytrap. See *Dionaea muscipula*
verbena, red, 39
Verbena bonariensis, 164, 184, 194, **195**, 201
Veronica austriaca 'Ionian Skies', 38
Viburnum rhytidophyllum, 139
viola, 71, 119, 120
violet, dog's-tooth. See *Erythronium californicum*
    'White Beauty'

Vitis 'Glenora', 95
Vitis 'Himrod', 95
Vitis 'Schuyler', 95
Vitis vinifera Black Hamburgh. See *Vitis vinifera* 'Schiava Grossa'
Vitis vinifera 'Schiava Grossa', 93, **94**, 199

wallflower, alpine, 38
watercress, 98
water forget-me-not. See *Myosotis scorpioides*
waterlily, 137, 139
waterweed, curly. See *Lagarosiphon major*

wax flower. See *Hoya carnosa*
whorled milfoil. See *Myriophyllum verticillatum*
wisteria, 40
woodrush, greater. See *Luzula sylvatica* 'Aurea'
wrinkled cress, 103

Yushania, 127

Zantedeschia, 77
zucchini. See courgette
Zygocactus, 71